How to Be a Lyft and Ub[...]
Driver's Manual
U.S. Copyright © 2018 W[...]
ISBN 9781686552007

Rideshare Business Guide
The author's website www.RideshareBusinessGuide.com is dedicated to helping new and existing rideshare drivers find meaningful answers to their rideshare driving questions.

Rideshare Drivers Mentoring/Coaching Program
The Rideshare Business Guide Mentoring Program provides one-on-one mentoring for new and established drivers. Through one-on-one mentoring (or just answering a few questions) new drivers are able to avoid or work through the struggles that Wylee encountered as a new driver. Wylee's ultimate goal is to help every new driver experience maximum financial success and minimum personal stress. Anyone referred by Wylee to sign up as a new driver with Uber or Lyft are never charged for this service.

Wylee's Rideshare Driving Book and Workbook
How to Be a Lyft and Uber Driver – The Unofficial Driver's Manual
Driving for Uber and Lyft - How Much Can Drivers Earn?
These non-fiction volumes share what Wylee learned about being a successful driver for Uber and Lyft in over three years of full-time rideshare driving. Each volume is dedicated to Wylee's goal of helping new and existing drivers be successful and not give up on what Wylee knows from personal experience is a viable way to earn meaningful income.

EARN CASH BONUSES FOR RECOMMENDING THIS BOOK
Rideshare Business Guide will work with individuals and business entities seeking to monetize promoting Wylee's rideshare driving books as well as the Rideshare Business Guide website.
Inquires send email to: admin@ridesharebusinessguide.com

Table of Contents

INTRODUCTION
WHAT IS THE "GIG" ECONOMY AND WHY YOU SHOULD CARE?

"Gig economy" = a labor market characterized by the prevalence of short-term contracts or freelance work as opposed to permanent jobs.

Rideshare driving (Uber/Lyft/Etc.) is a viable "gig" in the gig economy and rideshare driving will produce interesting average hourly income for rideshare drivers.

Rideshare driving part-time can be a relatively easy and even fun way to make supplemental income. Rideshare driving is also a job, and like most jobs comes with challenges for rideshare drivers.

Obviously part-time rideshare drivers will face some of the same "challenges" as full-time drivers; however, working part-time the challenges are likely to be easier to stomach as "part of the job." Before deciding rideshare driving will be your full-time gig it is important to recognize that doing anything 40+ hours every week is going to feel like "work" at least some of the time.

One significant challenge can be understanding the math required to calculate actual "Take Home Pay."

Even if the rideshare vehicle is not the most economical car/truck on the road, rideshare driving will always produce more income than expense. However, calculating "take home pay" requires determining the approximate expense of the depreciating resale value of the rideshare driving vehicle and estimating future maintenance and repair expenses. These topics are covered in detail in the book: Driving for Uber and Lyft - How Much Can Drivers Earn? available from www.RideshareBusinessGuide.com.

In this book, *How to Be a Lyft and Uber Driver – The Unofficial Driver's Manual* the focus is on the day-to-day aspects of the gig. One goal of this work is providing a detailed "roadmap" toward profitable and low-stress rideshare driving.

As independent contractors (not traditional employees) rideshare drivers don't get a manual from Uber or Lyft describing how to deal with unreasonable or difficult passengers or for that matter how to maximize rideshare driving profits.

Uber and Lyft do cover some important topics in their online trainings, but Uber and Lyft have to be very careful to not give the appearance of treating independent contractors as employees, so the online trainings do not cover important topics in detail. Also true, the independent contractor business model means Uber and Lyft online training may be skewed toward what is best for Uber and Lyft; possibly not best for the independent rideshare drivers.

With the goal of providing a safety net for new rideshare drivers this work: *How to Be a Lyft and Uber Driver – The Unofficial Driver's Manual* was created to assist new (and existing) rideshare drivers while they define how (as an independent contractor) they will approach the gig.

The second major challenge is what I call "the mental game" of rideshare driving. Rideshare driving can be mentally stressful for a number of reasons including: worrying about income – "what is my take home pay?"; being in close-quarters with challenging passengers; other cars on the road - traffic; pedestrians, bicycles, and skateboards (oh my); etc.

Working full-time for two years as a rideshare driver I've experienced challenges and wondered if some of the same challenges could help explain why traditional taxi drivers so often seem burnt out - maybe full-time taxi driving isn't an easy job?

As a rideshare driver with 11,000+ completed trips it's common to hear my passengers talk about past negative experiences traveling in traditional taxi cabs, experiences that have them favoring rideshare transportation. One of my passengers (a resident of Chicago visiting Denver) said: "*I think Chicago taxi drivers must be the unhappiest people on the planet.*"

My personal experience with traditional taxi transportation is limited to a few years of business travel but nothing I experienced suggested taxi drivers were a happy lot. Because flagging down an available taxi or calling a taxi company's 800 number never felt reliable to me - when I needed to be picked up on time and be transported efficiently, I scheduled a town-car service.

I could call a town-car service in advance and book a car to pick me up when I needed to go. Town-car service usually meant knowing my driver's name at least a day in advance: "*Ben will pick you up at the 1234 Main Street, Nortel office at 2:30 p.m. and take you to the Chicago O'Hare airport, United gates.*" My town-car drivers were always on time; well-dressed, courteous and the Lincoln Town Cars were immaculately clean.

Town-car services and traditional taxi businesses still exist; however, in the emerging gig economy their business models are challenged by the rideshare industry.

Transportation industry analysts project annual passenger trips in traditional taxis will continue to shrink while passenger trips in rideshare vehicles will continue to grow – good news for rideshare drivers!

One dramatic example of this trend, the value of a taxi "medallion" (required in most US cities, regulates and limits the number of legal taxis on the road) has plummeted in the past few years. In 2012, one of the 14,000+ New York City taxi medallions sold for $1.3 million dollars; then just five years later, in April of 2017, a NYC taxi medallion sold for $241,000.

TAXI

Important benefits of rideshare driving are the flexible work hours and considerably less financial "buy in" compared to traditional taxi driving. Since there are rideshare passenger Trip Requests 24 hours of the day rideshare drivers have 100% flexibility choosing when they drive.

With the rideshare driving gig going to work simply means going "Online" on the Uber/Lyft Driver smart phone applications; to stop working go "Offline" and the gig is over.

This flexibility comes with "a price."

The ability to go on and offline whenever you want sounds great because it is; however, the basic nature of transporting strangers in your personal car or truck takes a while to get used to and after a couple of "challenging" passenger experiences going back online can be more difficult than it sounds – this is exactly "the mental game" of rideshare driving.

Dealing with the mental game of being a rideshare driver is one of the reasons I wrote this book; I was determined to develop simple-to-follow plans to make my rideshare driving gig less stressful and more profitable and just as determined to not let a few "bad" passengers ruin the gig for me.

The flexibility of rideshare driving for the past two years has meant picking up my elementary-age kids at school at least three days a week. As a parent the "value" of standing outside my son's classroom door when the bells rings at 2:30 p.m. - most parents will understand me when I say: "Golden Times."

However, "The Price" of this flexibility is how easy it is to not work, not go "Online", not earn the income you hoped to make rideshare driving, and you will only have to look to the closest mirror to see who is responsible.

Let's get started and move to the matter of: "Getting Our Minds Right" which is an important first step for "rookie" rideshare drivers (and maybe some seasoned ones too?)

GET YOUR MIND RIGHT FOR RIDESHARE DRIVING...

"Success is peace of mind which is a direct result of self-satisfaction in knowing you did your best to become the best you are capable of becoming." John Wooden

Rideshare driving has an extremely high turnover rate meaning most people who try rideshare driving quit soon after they start.

Research suggests about fifty percent quit and never drive again less than 30 days after they start driving. Another fifty percent quit less than 90 days after they start, again quitting intending to never rideshare drive again. After one year, only 10-12 percent are still earning money transporting rideshare passengers.

To put these statistics another way, if we started with 100 new rideshare drivers only 50 are still on the road 30 days later. After 90 days only 25 of the original 100 drivers are still on the road rideshare driving. One-year after the 100 rideshare drivers started only 10-12 are still earning income rideshare driving.

Some of the fallout can be explained by the fact that rideshare driving is often a temporary gig, men and women earning rideshare driving until they return to other work – a transition job.

Another important reason rideshare drivers quit is rideshare passengers can sometimes be challenging and the new rideshare drivers haven't been prepared by the rideshare companies to "have their minds right." It's simply not in the rideshare company's interest to train new rideshare drivers to, for example, be prepared to "just say no" to unreasonable requests.

Every research article and rideshare driver blog report I've ever seen agrees that most rideshare passengers behave as if they appreciate the service rideshare drivers provide and behave as if they respect the fact that rideshare drivers are using their own cars/trucks to transport them to their destinations.

Only a small percentage of rideshare passengers behave in ways that are challenging, especially for new rideshare drivers. These passenger

4

experiences could make it easy to believe that rideshare driving is just not worth the hassle.

Personally, I spent months where I was often not enjoying my rideshare driving gig typically because my mind was thinking about "bad" passengers I might get on the next trip rather than appreciating the "good" or benign passengers currently in my car.

NINA'S ADVENTURES - "WHY I QUIT MY YOGA CLASS" by Nina Paley

If you take advantage of the information found in this book, it is extremely unlikely you will fall into the group that quits because of a few experiences with "bad" passengers. Armed with the information found here you will be far better prepared for the rideshare driving gig compared to the average new rideshare driver.

Another reason new rideshare drivers quit is they have never run their own business and the rideshare companies are not training how to do this either. These drivers quit questioning if the income they are earning is "fair" for the time spent rideshare driving. They also question if the income is sufficient to cover the current and future expenses of using their personal vehicle.

Rideshare company's advertisements use catchy phasing like: "The ultimate side gig" which doesn't sound like running your own business to me. I've seen posts in rideshare driving forums belittling participants using words like "career" and "business" to describe rideshare driving experiences.

Understanding that rideshare driving is a business is essential for drivers determined not to quit because they didn't feel prepared for the gig.

Honestly rideshare driving is not for everyone. If you try rideshare driving it is my personal hope you decide to continue rideshare driving or quit based on your personal reasons and not because you did not feel prepared.

To run a successful rideshare driving business it is most important to understand the business math. In order to feel "successful" you will need to understand how to calculate and prepare for rideshare driving expenses, including the cost of eventually replacing the car or truck you use for your rideshare driving gig.

Understanding the math means knowing how to calculate your actual "take home pay."

To prevent yourself from falling into this group get a copy of *Driving for Uber and Lyft - How Much Can Drivers Earn?* available from www.RideshareBusinessGuide.com. This guide provides the essential math and other tools required to understand and manage the income and expenses of running a rideshare driving business.

Before moving on to the next topic here are a few thoughts intended to help us all "get our minds right."

As a young man I read Dr. Norman Vincent Peale's book The Power of Positive Thinking. A great book but I'm not suggesting you should read it before getting out on the road as a new rideshare driver. Peale's book shaped the way I viewed the world and the thoughts helped me in countless ways for decades.

Recently I came across related articles describing a technique called: "Positive Neutrality" and what I read again changed the way I viewed the world and really helped me get my "mind right" as a rideshare driver and in my personal life.

I strongly recommend everyone read this article: *"Stop being positive and just cultivate neutrality for existential cool."*
https://tinyurl.com/ybeks2df

Staying neutral, what other articles refer to as: "Positive neutrality," is an extremely valuable "tool" for a rideshare driver.

While completing 11,000+ rideshare driving trips I've learned that while I would be hard-pressed to describe in detail the great conversations I had during my most recent day rideshare driving; I remember the "bad" trips in detail weeks, even months later.

Some psychologists believe our tendency to remember negative events more than positive ones is simply human nature.

Another great article: *"Praise Is Fleeting, but Brickbats We Recall"*
https://tinyurl.com/pbdfdmn

When I'm rideshare driving I work to cultivate thinking and acting/reacting from a neutral point of view. Since I am working to cultivate "positive neutrality" I'm not concerned when I'm having positive thoughts. Cultivating neutrality means I work to avoid labeling events as "negative" including: "bad" rideshare passengers; the behavior of other cars and trucks on the road; the behavior of pedestrians/bicyclers/skateboarders; how much money I'm earning on a given rideshare driving day; and any of the other events that could make my rideshare driving gig feel challenging.

Having our "minds right" for the rideshare driving gig is so important, in part because unlike a traditional "job" we decide when to get on the road – we don't have a boss wondering why you are not at work today.

In my experience it is too easy to decide to stay home and binge-watch my favorite shows rather than get out on the road and earn. This was true for me even though I was paying all of my monthly bills and rent solely with rideshare driving earnings.

If your rideshare driving earning goal is simply earning "extra" money imagine how easy it might be to stay home unless you have your "mind right?"

Author's Note: While working on writing Earn More, Stress Less I was also rideshare driving 40+ hours a week and of course thinking a lot about the contents of this book.

Because I was so focused on only writing what I not only believe... but also practice myself... I noticed there were times when I was not thinking or behaving in positive or neutral ways about the events in my rideshare driving days.

I realized I still have a way to go to have 100% neutral thinking and positive actions during my rideshare driving days. I will continue to work on this goal... and on the way to achieving the goal... I will endeavor to go easy on myself.

DEFINING YOUR "WHY" AND "WHAT"

"If you want to be happy, set a goal that commands your thoughts, liberates your energy and inspires your hopes." Andrew Carnegie

Before digging deeply into the day-to-day aspects of running your rideshare driving business let's continue to "Get our minds right" by thinking about two important questions:

1. WHY are you considering earning money as a rideshare driver?
2. WHAT other money-making options are available to you?

The importance of defining your unique answer to the question of "Why Drive" question can be a powerful motivator for the daily business of rideshare driving.

> **Making "extra" money...
> Rideshare Drive or something
> else?**

As a full-time rideshare driver I'm paying all of my bills with rideshare driving income and my daily/weekly/monthly earning goals are not measured by my average hourly earnings.

My earning goals are measured by how much money I need to pay my bills.

However, my average earning per hour tracked over hundreds of trips does help me determine approximately how many hours I need to drive each day/week/month to reach my earning goals.

My answer to the "Why Drive" question is easy – to pay all of my bills and personal expenses.

Part-time rideshare drivers drive for a variety of reasons: to make vacation money; pay for or offset the expense of owning a vehicle; fun money; pay a specific bill(s); etc.

By putting a dollar amount on your "Why Drive" answer it is easier to figure out approximately how many hours you will need to work to reach your personal earning goal.

Defining your personal "Why Drive" reason also makes it easier to motivate yourself to get on the road... after all it is always up to you!

By defining and focusing on "Why" you choose to be a rideshare driver you have the incentive to define and focus on your earning goal – the reason you choose to rideshare drive, the reason

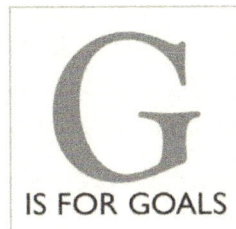

G

IS FOR GOALS

you get out on the road and earn despite the reality that you'd probably rather being doing something else.

Rideshare driving is not a difficult "job" but at least sometimes it's not an easy one either.

The second important question is "What".

Specifically, what are your other income earning options? Thinking for a moment only about hourly income what are your other options for making extra money or having a primary income source?

Defining my personal answer to the "Or What" question I used the formulas detailed in the book from www.RideshareBusinessGuide.com entitled: *Driving for Uber and Lyft - How Much Can Drivers Earn?* and know that replacing my full-time rideshare driving business income would take a job offering at least 40 hours a week and paying $18 to $20 an hour so $37,000 to $40,000 a year.

Obviously, some jobs come with benefits like discounted healthcare insurance and paid vacations but without understanding what I can make as a rideshare driver it would be difficult to make an informed decision to continue rideshare driving full-time or accept a full-time traditional job offer.

By defining your "Or What", you will be able to make informed decisions about how you earn "extra" money or enough money to pay all your bills.

To help motivate yourself to clearly define your "Why" and "What" answers read on.

UNDERSTANDING THE "LAW" OF AVERAGES

During my first college degree one of the courses I found most difficult was called "Quantitative Statistics in Psychological Theory" which was an introduction to a statistics course offered by the psychology department. While normally an A student I was very happy to complete that statistics course with B... statistics is a complicated but powerful subject.

"The law of averages is the law that a particular outcome or event is inevitable or certain simply because it is statistically possible.

Depending on context or application it can be considered a valid common-sense observation or a misunderstanding of probability.

This notion can lead to fallacious thinking [based on a mistaken belief] when one becomes convinced that a particular outcome must come soon simply because it has not occurred recently (e.g. believing that because three consecutive coin flips yielded heads, the next coin flip must be virtually guaranteed to be tails)."

(https://en.wikipedia.org/wiki/Law_of_averages)

Reading and attempting to fully comprehend this definition still makes my brain hurt a little but I clearly remember at the beginning of the statistics course the professor going on and on about flipping coins.

The "nut" if you will, is if you were to flip a coin a sufficient number of times the end result will be an equal number of "heads" and "tails" outcomes. Since there are only two possible outcomes, heads or tails, with enough flips of a coin the average outcome will be an even number of heads and tails results.

The law of averages is an important concept for a rideshare driver. As an example, just because I haven't recently had a Trip Request for a long trip doesn't mean there is a better chance that one of my next trips will be a long one. On the other hand, **when I look at my earnings over a week or month or months, etc. my average earnings per hour on the road have been very consistent.**

The book _Driving for Uber and Lyft - How Much Can Drivers Earn?_ from www.RideshareBusinessGuide.com references my Rideshare Earning Case Study detailing my daily/weekly/monthly average earnings reports for the 2017 & 2018 calendar years, the data I collected makes clear despite the variability of my income from one rideshare driving day to the next my average hourly earnings over time are consistent.

If you don't already have a copy of the case study send an email to wylee@ridesharebusinessguide.com and request a copy.

So even though I am disappointed and sometimes struggle to remain neutral in my thinking, when my average earnings on a given work day are lower than my overall average I know that over time the short, medium, and long trips as well as rideshare companies Surge Pricing, Promotions, and Bonuses will all average out to be $16-$18 an hour driving during the day and $20-$22 driving in the late afternoon, evening, and late night.

Knowing that my rideshare earnings average out over time makes it easier for me to stick to my rideshare driving gig when my average hourly earnings are low and not wonder if I should looking harder for a traditional job.

Another related thought; according to articles I've read online most rideshare drivers work part-time and are on the road earning 10-15 hours a week. Although I have not diligently tracked the number of average trips I complete per hour, when I look at my trip history for a given day of driving I usually average 2 – 2.5 trips per hour on the road. This means working only 10-15 hours a week a part-time driver will complete about 20-30 trips per week. Working full-time, average 40 hours a week, I'm completing 80+ trips.

An important point I want to make here: taking the law of averages into account a full-time driver will likely experience more of everything more quickly when compared to a part-time driver.

If you choose to be a rideshare driver and work part-time you might experience a day or two of lower earnings and there might be days of not driving between the two lower earning days. Instead of getting discouraged remember; rideshare driving earnings will average out over time, it just may take longer to determine your personal average hourly earnings when driving part-time.

On the other hand, if you are driving part-time and focus on getting on the road during the higher average higher earning nights and weekends, over time your average earnings might be a bit higher than mine.

Also true, if you are focused on daytime driving and using rideshare company's application features to limit the types of trips you are offered (for example only getting rides in a defined part of town) your average hourly earnings might be less when compared to mine.

My mom, a retired accountant, once pointed out:

"The law of averages, it's not just a good idea... it is a law."

SUCCEEDING AT RIDESHARE DRIVING

"One important key to success is self-confidence. An important key to self-confidence is preparation." Arthur Ashe

To succeed at rideshare driving it will help to consider this: there are three major players in the emerging world of rideshare transportation each of which is motivated to pursue different primary goals... rideshare drivers want to make money; rideshare passengers want to get where they are going; and the rideshare companies (Transportation Network Company or TNC) want to maximize market share meaning attracting and retaining rideshare passengers and rideshare drivers.

If you choose to be a rideshare driver it may sometimes seem like the TNCs are prioritizing passenger's experience over driver satisfaction; this may seem short-sited however their 10 to 20-year business goals include all but eliminating the rideshare driver with self-driving cars and trucks.

Reading optimistic media stories, it may seem a driverless future is just around the corner.

The robot cars will have to clear a number of significant barriers before they displace rideshare drivers, primarily passenger acceptance. Before I'm ready to ride around town in a car with no one behind the wheel millions of accident-free passenger trips will have already been completed.

Another significant barrier to wide-spread use of robot cars: for the same reason it is expensive for a TNC to "open" a new city it will be expensive and time-consuming to roll out driverless cars for rideshare.

To open a new city there must be lots of drivers at all times of day, so passengers can count on the service; and until there are a lot of passengers driver's income will have to be significantly subsidized. Magnify this reality by a factor of at least 10 and you will be able to imagine the state of robot cars taking over the work rideshare drivers do today... passengers have to be willing to accept robot cars and trucks before it will make business sense to invest in the technology.

Without a doubt the current TNCs, like Uber and Lyft, will invest early and aggressively promote progress towards a driverless future, but it will be many years before robot cars are a viable replacement for rideshare drivers.

My point: I'm not worried about a robot taking away my rideshare driving income and if you decide to be a rideshare driver neither should you.

So "no worries, mate" – if you choose to give rideshare driving forget about the robot cars and focus on your rideshare driving primary goal, to make money!

While you are making money rideshare driving it will help you to understand the primary goals of the other players in the rideshare industry. By understanding and accepting "what is" you will avoid some of the challenging aspects of being a rideshare driver.

When you find yourself expending unnecessary emotional energy and your time on anything other your primary goal, making money, you will be able to recognize unhelpful thoughts and refocus your thinking.

> **PRIMARY MOTIVATORS**
>
> RIDESHARE DRIVERS = MAKE MONEY
>
> RIDESHARE PASSENGERS = SAFE TRANSPORTATION
>
> RIDESHARE COMPANIES = SECURE MARKETSHARE

This book, *How to Be a Lyft and Uber Driver – The Unofficial Driver's Manual*, documents things I wish I knew before my first trip as a rideshare driver and what I have figured out during my 11,000+ completed rideshare driving trips.

To pursue the goal of making money as a rideshare driver it also helps to understand rideshare driver "take home pay" simply calculated as income minus expenses. This book, *How to Be a Lyft and Uber Driver – The Unofficial Driver's Manual*, does not go in depth on that topic.

To understand the financial aspects of running a rideshare driving business get a copy of the book from www.RideshareBusinessGuide.com entitled Driving for Uber and Lyft - How Much Can Drivers Earn? which provides all the information you need to manage the income and expenses of running your own rideshare driving business and therefore calculate rideshare diving "take home pay."

For now, let's return our focus to primary goals and why they are so important to rideshare driving success.

Your primary goal as a rideshare driver is making money, simple and straight-forward.

The rideshare passenger's primary goal is to get a ride from Point A to Point B.

Sometimes passenger's behavior will suggest they may be (at least unconsciously) pursuing additional goals. The contents of this book will help you understand what to expect and how to react (or not) when passengers are less than respectful.

Most passengers will be easy and clearly focused on their primary goal; they will behave in a respectful manner – **when rideshare passengers are less than easy the rideshare driver chooses how to react - or if to react at all.**

If you choose to be a rideshare driver remember your primary goal is to make money; everything else is secondary.

Understanding the TNC's (Transportation Network Companies) primary goal is more complicated. You might be surprised to hear that in 2018-2019 being a profitable company is probably not the TNC's current primary goal.

For the present and immediate future, the TNCs are losing billions of dollars every year and are kept alive by private investors gambling they will eventually get a healthy return on their investments.

In the high-tech, gig economy world selling a company's stock on the public market is much easier than becoming a profitable company especially when a company is offering a "Disruptive Technology."

As a rideshare driver it is logical, and I believe helpful, to always have in your thinking that a future public stock offering is the most likely primary goal the TNC's are currently pursuing.

A past example of this reality - Amazon lost billions of dollars for years, to many people including me, Amazon's business model did not make sense. Venture capital investors bet that Amazon's "Disruptive Technology" would win in the long run... and the investors were proved right.

After years of losing money Amazon became a profitable company and is currently the #1 retail "store" in the United States with annual gross revenue over $100 billion dollars.

The TNCs are able to lose money year after year because investors are spending (investing) a lot of money hoping for the same kind of investment "home run."

To emphasize this point, it is logical to think that day-to-day activities of the TNCs are managed toward this primary goal in part because every member of the TNC's senior management (and many management levels down) will personally profit handsomely when the TNC has a public stock offering.

As rideshare drivers it is logical for us to assume TNC management is making decisions about

> In January of 2018 Japanese company SoftBank made a private investment in Uber and the former CEO Travis Kalanick sold 10% of his stock options for $1.4 billion dollars.
>
> This means just one member of Uber's senior management still holds stock options valued at over $12 billion dollars.

daily operations toward the primary goal of a public stock offering and all other goals are secondary unless they are seen to support the primary goal.

To support the goal of taking the company public the TNC's are working to maximize market share by attracting and retaining passengers and drivers... a larger market share means greater initial public stock (IPO) offering value.

This means discounted or even free rides for passengers; bonuses for drivers; and regular promotions that increase active driver's income – all significant business expenses that do not help the TNC's become profitable.

Clarifying the TNC's primary goal is important for a rideshare driver to understand because there will be times when a TNC's actions don't seem to make sense.

When a TNC's actions don't seem to make sense remember that the TNC's primary goal is currently not being a profitable company, the current goal is capturing market share (passengers and drivers) and taking the company public through an IPO.

After the IPO keeping the stock price stable and moving up will become the new primary goal.

It is also helpful to understand a little about how the TNCs work internally, why the TNCs do what they do; know that the TNCs employ hundreds of professionals with psychology backgrounds. Their job it is to develop programs and processes that will attract and retain passengers and drivers therefore increasing the TNC's market value.

The rideshare industry relies on people, passengers and drivers, and in order to grow it makes business sense to motivate people to embrace rideshare transportation. These psychology professionals significantly contribute to the job of motivating passengers and drivers to do things that support the TNC's current primary goal and future viability.

The input from these psychology professionals is used to create incentive programs for passengers and drivers. Since rideshare drivers are independent contractors the TNCs cannot tell drivers when and where to work and must instead rely on promotions with financial incentives to motivate drivers.

No doubt these promotions have added to my personal rideshare driving income, but I've learned to make my own decisions about when and where to work often ignoring an active promotion.

In my first few months as a rideshare driver I sometimes felt the TNCs and rideshare passengers were not always being entirely honest with me and these thoughts were not helpful in my day-to-day rideshare driving activities or personal peace of mind.

Almost two years and over 11,000 trips later I am less likely to feel "manipulated" by the TNCs or my passengers – I am focused on my primary goal of making money rather than putting my energy and focus into things that really aren't that important.

If you choose to be a rideshare driver – when you are working with rideshare passengers and the TNCs I strongly suggest you keep your actions as simple as possible and stay focused on your primary goal. Rideshare driving is a great way to earn non-trivial income and anything that does not contribute to making money is not worthy of your focus or your energy.

FIRST DO NO HARM

"Life without hope is hopelessly difficult but at the end hope can so easily make fools of us all." ~Henry Marsh

"First do no harm" is part of the Hippocratic Oath; part of medical school education. In the case of rideshare driving I use this phrase to remind myself how important it is to aggressively avoid getting traffic tickets, getting into an accident, or doing anything that that will cause me financial or other harm.

Some rideshare drivers won't know that overloading their vehicles with passengers; or transporting a small child without an appropriate car-seat or booster; or letting the front-seat passenger ride without a seat belt; or violating regulations related to rideshare driving is also risking a traffic ticket or regulatory fine. In the case of child car seats, a criminal charge.

"Risk comes from not knowing what you're doing." ~Warren Buffett

Typically, I drive about the same speed as the surrounding traffic, within reason of course. In most cases I am not the fastest car on the road, but I will typically drive a mile or two above posted speed limit when I have a passenger in the car. I figure I'm delivering a service, so I drive the way I would normally drive when I want to be at my personal destination as soon as safely and legally as possible. In other words, I always drive safely but unless my passenger said: "Please drive slow so I can watch the grass grow…" I drive like I am delivering a service efficiently as possible.

I am incredibly cautious when I drive and think: "*Any car and truck around my car is capable of doing anything at any given moment.*"

When I am starting out from a traffic light I make darn sure there is not a dump truck clearly about to run the red light. By rideshare driving you are driving more miles, so statistically you are more likely to get a ticket or be involved in an accident - safety first always.

When I have passengers in my car I always use my turn signals, if the passenger is paying attention the turn signal tells them we are on track to their destination. I'm so diligent with my turn signals I sometimes find myself using them in an apartment parking lot and thinking: "*That was unnecessary?*"

Having a goal to "Do No Harm," means never giving a police officer an easy reason to pull my car over.

I always assume there may be a police car watching my every move and I'm always thinking:

"As a full-time rideshare driver I am driving considerably more miles so far more likely to get a traffic ticket if I am always pushing limits and taking risks."

DAY TO DAY STUFF...

WHAT DOES RIDESHARE DRIVING "LOOK" LIKE?

Of course, the closest job comparison to rideshare driving is professional taxi driver; however, it's not a perfect example.

Traditional taxi drivers don't hand out free water or mints; typically, they won't offer a charger for your phone; or care what music they are playing; or about the cleanliness and smell of the cars they drive.

Unless you are very lucky a traditional taxi driver is unlikely to invite you to sit in the front seat while they listen attentively to you yammer on about whatever is on your mind today. (To be fair while rideshare driving I have enjoyed most of the conversations I've had with well over 15,000 strangers - although sometimes my throat gets dry from talking so much.)

And taxi drivers are famous all over the world for driving unsafely with passengers in their cars.

Countless times my passengers have told me about taxi rides where they were relieved to have survived the trip and walked away without being involved in an accident. My passengers have also said that in their experience taxi drivers are starting and stopping their cars roughly as if there was no one in the car but themselves.

Once a passenger told me he believed the taxi drivers in his home city, Chicago, had to be the unhappiest human beings on the planet.

Unhappiest human beings... this is an interesting thought when deciding if rideshare driving is for you?

Think about it for a second, why do traditional taxi drivers often seem indifferent or even upset about something or even everything?

After months of rideshare driving I realized some of the reasons why taxi drivers may not be enjoying their jobs.

Unless they make the decision to not react/respond there is something to be frustrated about essentially every moment of every day.

> *"Traffic is terrible."*

> *"Passengers are rude."*

> *"Pedestrians are idiots, it's amazing more of them aren't run over by cars every day."*

> *"I'm not getting good rides today, not making enough money."*

> *"My cab needs maintenance/repairs."*

The point: rideshare driving is not "hard" work but sometimes it doesn't feel "easy" either. Transporting strangers in your personal car for pay is not an experience many of us would call "normal" and rideshare drivers are running their own mini-business, something they may know little or nothing about.

My best suggestion is go easy on yourself, I've been rideshare driving for two years and there are still times when I feel uncomfortable doing the gig or get frustrated while on the job.

The basic nature of the "job" is simple:

1. Find the rideshare passengers pick-up location (where we hope they will be)
2. Transport them safely to their drop-off location

So, the gig is simple, make a choice to focus on the basic nature of the gig, and remember your primary goal is making money and everything else is secondary.

PASSENGER AND DRIVER STAR RATING?

Driver's star rating is based on the last 500 rated trips, if you have less than 500 trips the rating will be an average of all your rated trips. When you have more than 500 trips low passenger ratings will eventually rotate out of your average.

I don't worry about my rideshare driver star rating.

At least 50 passengers would have to give me a one-star rating to lower my average star rating low enough to risk be disconnected from the TNC application.

With an average star rating of 4.6 or less a driver runs the risk of essentially getting "fired" from the rideshare driving gig.

But have no fear... unless a driver does something seriously wrong the TNC's support organization will communicate and work with the driver before they are at risk for being disconnected.

If my driver star rating is 4.83 instead of 4.9 no one is going to care except maybe me. Passengers are not going to cancel a Trip Request because of a driver's star rating, the want a ride, if I'm the closest driver great.

I believe most of my passengers give me five stars or don't bother to rate me because:

- I am always polite, courteous, and behave professionally
- I focus on the road, drive safely while driving efficiently to the passenger's drop-off location
- My car is always mostly clean (more on this later)

In my thinking the TNC's star rating system for passengers and drivers isn't particularly relevant; at least not to my primary goal of making money rideshare driving.

Drivers rate every passenger's trip; passengers are never required to rate their drivers.

A passenger's star rating is an average of all their lifetime trips; however, drivers are not told how many total trips a passenger has taken, this means the number cannot be determined to be statistically significant, this fact makes passenger ratings less useful for drivers, or even not relevant at all.

A passenger with a 5-star rating might have taken only one trip!

I rate almost every passenger five stars, a passenger with only one lifetime trip who had me as their only driver is a five-star passenger... cool for them but about as relevant as my "new high score" in the Panda Pop game I play on my phone when I'm bored.

A passenger with a 4.4 star rating might have only five lifetime trips: three five stars, one four star, and one three star rating – do the math, this averages to a 4.4 star rating.

In this example imagine the driver who gave the passenger three stars rates every passenger three stars if they take over two minutes to get into his car. The driver who gave the passenger 4 stars gives almost all his passengers 4 stars, his reasoning is unknown.

Drivers receive almost no direction from the TNC how to use the star rating system, so each driver uses his own criteria for passenger ratings.

Think about this reality for a second; since the TNC's do not provide guidance what the star ratings mean, <u>every driver and every passenger uses the star rating system the way they think it should be used.</u>

It is impossible to find statistically-relevant data points in a dataset which was collected using a completely random process.

<u>Now think about this:</u> A driver could be disconnected from the driver application for having a 4.6 star rating in their past 500 passenger rated trips, that would mean any passenger who rates a driver 4 stars or less is essentially saying the driver should be fired?

Obviously, most passengers are not rating drivers 4 stars because they think they should be fired, only a few passengers are aware drivers could be "fired" for having a 4.6 star rating, the ones who are aware of this probably rate every driver 5 stars...

If a passenger really thought a driver should be fired, they should rate the driver 1 star? Makes sense?

In the example of the passenger with the 4.4 star rating, if I knew that passenger had 100 lifetime trips his 4.4 star rating would be a statistically relevant number, as a driver I might hesitate to pick them up.

Most drivers I've talked to do the same thing I do: "I give most passengers five stars."

It would be interesting to know how many 3-star ratings a passenger had received, of course to be meaningful information I would also have to also know how many lifetime trips the passenger had taken.

Most drivers eventually learn that rating a passenger 3 stars or less means the TNC application will not match them with that passenger for a future trip.

As a rideshare driver if I knew a passenger had essentially been rejected for future trips by lots of drivers, that is probably a passenger I'd rather not have in my car?

But drivers don't know how many lifetime trips a passenger has taken, which makes a passenger's star rating not relevant; or at least not relevant to me.

So, I don't pay attention to passenger star ratings and I never have. And unless the star rating system is someday changed significantly, I will continue to not pay attention to passenger star ratings.

With driver's star rating, the only relevant aspect to a knowledgeable driver, is they could be disconnected from the TNC driver application if their average rating falls below about 4.6 stars.

But again, not as relevant as you might think, because the TNC will communicate with a driver with a low star rating and work with the driver before disconnecting them. Unless a driver does something significantly bad, as example a passenger communicates the driver seemed to be under the influence of drugs or alcohol, it is not in the TNC's interest to have less drivers on the road.

My star rating is always 4.9(something) stars with Uber and Lyft, this rating is based on my last 500 rated trips. I've done the math and it would take almost 50 one-star ratings to pull my average score to 4.6 stars.

Another interesting reality to contemplate, imagine for a moment if I became so disgruntled with rideshare driving and was taking out my frustration on my passengers... it would take about 50 passengers rating me one-star before the TNC support organization contacted me about my star rating?

Imagine how many three or two-star ratings it would take to lower my currently stellar star rating low enough to risk being disconnected from the TNC driver application?

Can you say: "The star rating system, as it is currently deployed, is really not relevant to passengers or drivers?"

Another interesting statistic, most of my passengers, less than half, do not bother to rate their trips in my car.

I imagine I will always get an occasional 4-star rating. I believe some passengers fancy themselves rideshare connoisseurs and only give a 5-star rating if a driver happens to accidentally do whatever they expect from a 5-star driver.

If I knew a passenger, as example, expected me to engage them in interesting conversation in order to earn a 5-star rating instead of a 4-star rating, I might behave differently, but probably not, my primary rideshare driving goal is to make money not attempting to satisfy expectations that are not communicated by the occasional rideshare passenger who fancies themselves a connoisseur of rideshare transportation.

It is unlikely I will get many ratings lower than 4 stars primarily because I'm willing to say: "No" to passengers when it is obvious at the pick-up location they will not be respectful passengers. (More on this later)

If a driver never chooses "Start Trip" in the TNC driver application then a passenger cannot rate the driver. It's ironic I think, a passenger who expected me to allow an open-topped plastic cup containing an alcoholic beverage in my car might rate me 4-stars because I didn't [fill in the blank uncommunicated metric]?

Another reason I believe it is unlikely I will get many lower-than-four-star passenger ratings, when the rare passenger misbehaves while in my car, I probably ignored the behavior, or I played along knowing after the trip ends I will rate them 3 stars or less and never see them again.

My thinking and approach to the TNC's star rating systems is not my choice really, the TNC's poor implementation of their star rating system drives my behavior, just not the way the TNC probably intended.

It can be emotionally satisfying to give a passenger three stars or less. If I give a passenger three stars or less after the trip is over, I will never be matched with them again.

In over 11,000 trips I've only rated a handful of passengers three stars or less; and every time I have, it has felt good knowing I will never be matched with the passenger again.

When a passenger brings up the rating system in conversation, I have asked if they would cancel on a driver with a lower rating, every passenger has responded with some version of: *"No, I want a ride and don't pay much attention to a driver's star rating."*

The only time I hear passengers talking about a driver's average star rating is when they say something like: "*You know you have a 4.98-star rating and over 9,000 Uber trips?*"

I never bring up the topic of the TNC's star rating system, if the topic does come up, whatever a passenger believes about their personal star rating I usually let them continue to believe.

I don't train passengers for future rides and am not willing to introduce a topic with the potential to start a negative conversation. (More about this later)

As I said, I rate almost every passenger five stars. Occasionally I will give a four-star rating, most often because I traveled more than five minutes to reach the pick-up location and then waited another five minutes at the curb before the passenger got into my car. If I only have to drive a couple of minutes to the pick-up location I am less likely to care about spending a few minutes at the curb.

It's still rude for passengers to make a rideshare driver wait more than a minute at the curb, passengers wave down traditional taxis are standing at the curb ready to get into the taxi and go where they are going… even in the rain or snow.

I might also give a four-star rating if the passenger's actions while in my car have felt abrasive to me, blatantly rude or way outside what I believe are societal norms.

Interesting I think, it's common for me to think about giving a passenger a four-star rating then by the end of the ride I forget and give them five stars, it is easy to forget something I don't believe is relevant.

I've never given a passenger a two star rating, my thinking: "*What's the point?*" What would I be trying to communicate, and to who?

If a TNC's star rating system somehow gave more "weight" to a passenger who received a two-star rating from a driver who gives almost every passenger five-stars… that might lead to some relevant data-points… but again unless the TNCs gave drivers more information, then again… irrelevant.

If I give a passenger a one-star rating, I always open a written support ticket documenting what happened. If I've given a passenger a one-star rating, my support ticket sometimes says I believe the passenger's behavior was so bad they should be suspended for a week or more from requesting rides.

Passengers can be banned for 24 hours, a week, or even longer if their behavior in your car seriously violates the contract the customer agreed to when they registered a passenger account with the TNC.

I take the time to write a support ticket because I believe there is a greater potential for the passenger I just rated one-star to write a complaint about me, I'm expecting lies or half-truths from the passenger about what happened, I always behave in a professional manner.

I open a support ticket because when support hears the passenger's story, I want my side of the experience to already be on record. The passenger's story might not be entirely truthful, and I think my version will be deemed more credible because I've been proactive and my report doesn't sound like a defensive response to a passenger's lies or half-truths.

In the restaurant industry people who habitually complain about something hoping to get the meal "comped" or at least reduced in price are known by insiders as: "Gypsies."

The same kind of thing can happen with rideshare transportation, a passenger complains about a driver hoping to get a refund or cheaper rides in the future.

Final thoughts on the star rating systems... there are a few things I do with every ride with the goal of making every passenger's ride a "Five Star Trip":

- **I am polite and professional in all my communications.**
    - I never use profanity and I take care to be as neutral as possible about almost everything that happens.
    - I don't volunteer stories about "bad" passengers. If asked, I make sure my description of events is based on the facts and let the audience make their own value judgements.

- **I ALWAYS confirm the passenger name** on the Trip Request before I select "Start Trip" and always confirm the passenger's **drop-off destination address** after I select "Start Trip."
    - In over 11,000 trips confirming the name and destination has only solved a few issues – if I were not behaving in a professional manner it would be easy to skip or gloss over this step.
    - If you watch driver's YouTube videos you will see some drivers skipping this step and risking the possible

consequences... more important they don't look like professions.

- o Confirming the name and destination at the pick-up location communicates with my actions that I approach rideshare driving in a professional manner.

- **I always keep my eyes on the road and always drive safely.**
  - o Passengers don't know my driving skills when they enter my car, so I don't follow cars too closely, I always use my turn signals, and I make sure I don't do other things that might have passengers questioning my driving skills or willingness to diligently pay attention to the road.
  - o I almost never cross multiple lanes of traffic at the same time, sometimes this means a slightly longer trip, but it also means a safer trip.
  - o Basically, I drive as if my driver's education teacher, Mr. Blackburn, were in the car evaluating my driving.

- **My goal is to get to the passenger's drop-off location as quickly as possible without taking any risks, including not getting a ticket.**
  - o I typically move with the flow of traffic, if I were to get pulled over by a police car, the trip will take longer.
  - o I enjoy watching the flow of traffic and changing lanes only when I believe it will save time, it's like a game to see how well I can anticipate the flow of traffic and ever-changing conditions. If I look ahead and see a solid line of cars and trucks in every lane, it probably does not make sense to change lanes. On the other hand, if I know I have a few miles to travel on a busy highway before my exit it probably makes sense to move away from the "slow lane."

- **I think about being a good "party guest."**
  - o If the passenger wants to talk, I talk. If they seem to want to be quiet, I'm quiet.
  - o If we are talking, I try not to dominate the conversation. When people talk to bartenders or barber/hairdressers, they typically want to talk about themselves, so I let them.
  - o If there are multiple passengers or if a solo passenger is talking on the phone, I try not to insert myself into the conversation or otherwise make it obvious I heard everything they said. I say "try" because I'm not

26

always successful; sometimes what is said in my car is just too good not to comment or laugh.

- o If a passenger traveling solo sits in the front seat I assume they want to engage in conversation. If that passenger starts the conversation I talk about the topics they introduce. If I have to I'll bring up a topic, I'm willing to put some effort into making the conversation flow but not willing to work really hard, it's rare but sometimes I have passengers in the front seat and we are mostly quiet during the trip. (More on passenger conversations later)

- I play music chosen because the songs are popular, or at least they were when they were new, the songs I choose for my playlists are or were mainstream.
  - o Since most of the songs I play are from the 1980s & 1990s, it is accurate to say the songs I play "were" popular at the time. I'm not "hip" on the latest music, it's not my personal goal to be "hip", and know I don't have to be, I figure why spend energy on anything unless there is a very good chance I will make significantly more money?
  - o More on music in the next section, for now, know that I mostly play songs that have withstood the test of time, if people liked a song years ago it's likely people will enjoy hearing it today. In my car, very common to hear: "Wow, I haven't heard this song in a long time!" Then it's common for them to sing along.

With Lyft and Uber my current star rating as a driver is very high, I guess what I am doing works? It works for me anyway, rideshare drivers are independent and get to choose how they behave in their cars.

The way I manage my rideshare driving trips works for me because it is a reflection of who I am, my best advice is be yourself... or maybe the best possible version of yourself.

RIDESHARE PASSENGER TIPPING... OR NOT?

When I started rideshare driving, I thought that passing out waters and mints; or being an entertaining conversation participant; or basically anything I could think of to go the "extra mile" would equate to receiving tips from passengers.

Frankly, I was surprised to find out that in the short history of rideshare, it's only been around for a few years, almost no one tips rideshare drivers apparently no matter what the driver does to "earn" a tip. In 2018-19 more passengers are tipping but it's still true most passengers will not add a tip.

At rideshare driving events I have heard drivers say they get more tips because they bring up the topic of tipping to their passengers. This technique might work but just not my style. Maybe I'm leaving "money on the table" but I don't want to spend my days feeling like I'm "begging" for tips.

I spent months out on the road resenting the reality that almost no one tips rideshare drivers; and if you are like me and almost always tip when you buy a coffee or a sandwich, etc. it may be hard to understand why people would not tip a rideshare driver.

Take a look at the example to the right showing most of the trips I completed on Christmas Day 2017.

When I got out on the road Christmas afternoon I was optimistic I would receive some tips. But if people aren't going to tip a rideshare driver on Christmas Day I think we still have a way to go before tipping becomes commonplace in the rideshare experience.

On Christmas Day I heard lots of "Happy Holiday" greetings and the like... and one very nice couple gave me a wrapped slice of fancy bleu-cheese (It was awesome!) but tipping was like every other day... dismal.

Daily Earnings	
MONDAY, 12/25	
$128.41	
Trip Earnings	$115.56
Includes Surge, Boost, and tolls	
Toll	$11.85
Tips	$1.00
Total Daily Earnings	**$128.41**
3hr 47min	8
TIME ONLINE	TRIPS

Earnings Help

TRIPS

11:05 PM uberPOOL	$5.11
10:16 PM uberPOOL	$15.98
10:04 PM uberPOOL	$8.14
9:34 PM uberPOOL	$12.64 $11.64 + $1.00 Tip
9:01 PM uberPOOL	$21.83
7:57 PM uberX	$60.96
7:34 PM uberPOOL	$3.75

In 2017 I also drove on Thanksgiving Day and New Year's Eve with similar results, a couple of tips but mostly not.

Hopefully these examples will make it easier for you to not expect a lot of tips; and more importantly I suggest you not knock yourself out to

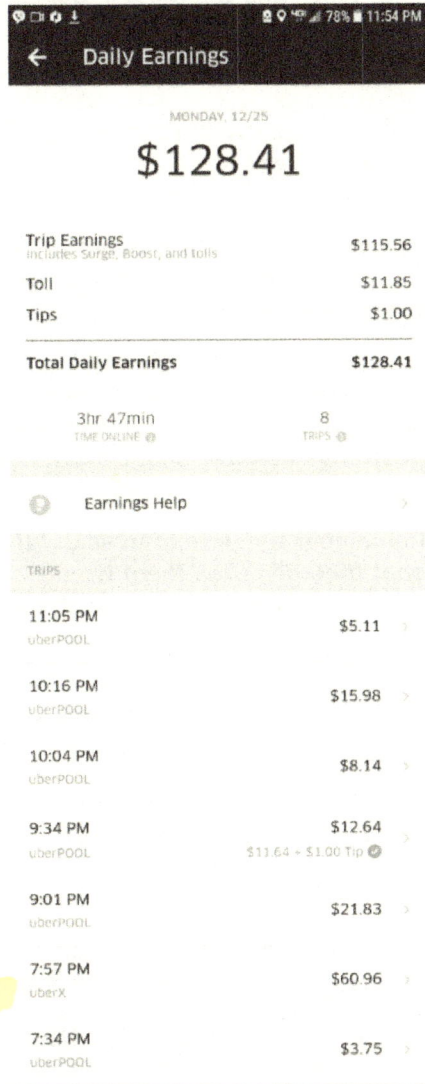

"earn" tips by offering bottled water and mints; trying to craft a perfect speech to deliver at the beginning of each ride; worrying about what kind of music you should be playing for a given passenger; basically I suggest you not strive to be "The best rideshare driver ever!"

Be polite, be professional, but be yourself and remember your car is your office and the most important person to please in your office... is you!

PASSENGER TIPPING – Part Two

If you're not striving to earn tips, how might that effect the way you approach the rideshare driving gig?

When I'm rideshare driving I'm the best version of "Me" who is also a rideshare driver.

In other words, I'm not striving to be any stereotype of a rideshare driver. I strive to be the best of myself and as neutral as possible about events that I could believe were "bad."

Remember the wise man said: *"If you don't want people getting your goat then don't tell them where you tied it up."* In other words, try not to let your passengers know if you are "bugged" by their behavior.

This tipping (or not) reality is true in part because the dominate Transportation Network Company (TNC) in the United States, Uber, trained people for years that tipping was not part of the rideshare transaction and people became accustomed to not leaving a tip when they rideshare.

The TNC, Lyft, had in-application tipping from the beginning, and when I added Lyft to my rideshare driving business, I was hopeful I would receive tips when completing Lyft trips.

After a month or so running Uber and Lyft applications it became clear most Lyft passengers weren't tipping me either.

Turns out most people have Uber and Lyft passenger applications loaded on their phones. Rideshare fares are not set by city ordinance like taxi fares. Rideshare passengers often compared current pricing before requesting a trip.

There is little customer loyalty to a specific TNC, most rideshare passengers are looking for the lowest price trip and if they don't leave a tip on Uber trips it's unlikely they will leave a tip when traveling with Lyft.

In the second half of 2017 Uber adding in-application tipping, an important, symbolic action to help legitimize rideshare tipping in passenger's minds. Now Uber passengers have a path to tip their drivers through the passenger application.

More frequent passenger tipping is currently the rideshare driver's best chance at increased average income.

Interestingly when Uber essentially founded the rideshare industry, rideshare trip fares were at least double what they are now meaning rideshare drivers were making considerably more money for every passenger trip. The higher fares also meant that tipping (or rather not tipping) was not as much of an issue.

Now with the ongoing fare wars, in America primarily between Uber and Lyft, it is unlikely the TNCs will be increasing passenger fares anytime soon.

Personally, I don't plan to change the way I approach my rideshare driving hoping to earn more tips, but I will continue to hope that rideshare passenger tipping will increase over time.

So, the point? If I had my "mind right" about tipping before I started rideshare driving I could have avoided months of mental "funk" because people were not tipping despite my efforts to be "The best rideshare driver they ever had."

> Once I picked up two passengers on a really hot day obviously just off a big hike in the Foothills so I cranked up the AC and offered them bottles of water as soon as they were settled in the backseat. I didn't do this because I was expecting a tip and frankly don't remember if a got one... I offered the waters because I feel good when I believe I am providing a better than average Rideshare Passenger experience.

The non-tipping reality also helped me make some important decisions about my behavior while rideshare driving and dramatically reduced the amount of emotional and physical energy I was expending.

Specifically, I decided that if most people aren't going to tip:

- I will listen to the music I want to hear... I create playlists containing songs I hope most people will enjoy, or at least not hate, but I'm the one sitting in my vehicle for hours and I'm going to listen to music I enjoy.

- I don't worry about holding up more than my end of conversations. Becoming comfortable with silence/not talking is still sometimes a challenge for me but when I notice feeling uncomfortable, I remind myself; my primary goal is making money; it is unlikely this passenger will leave a tip because of the conversations we have; and I get paid for transporting rideshare passengers from Point A to Point B not for entertaining them with my jokes and clever conversation on the way.

- I keep water and mints in my car however I typically don't offer my water/mints unless someone asks or if I hear someone say: "*I'm so thirsty*" or similar. I've long since given up thinking because a passenger received a free water or mint that they would leave a tip.

The primary point of this section is, as a rideshare driver I choose how I behave, and my actions are never about trying to "earn" a tip.

After all I'm not an employee I am a business owner... a distinction rideshare drivers should always have in mind when they are out on the road.

THE FRONT SEAT OF YOUR RIDESHARE DRIVING VEHICLES

More than a few passengers are going to want to ride in your front seat, some will ask if it's ok with you, but most will just get in the front seat without asking.

During the same months I was resenting the reality that most passengers do not tip, I also spent about two months politely requesting that passengers ride in the backseat, unless there were at least three passengers traveling in the trip.

Before arriving at the pick-up location, I would unlock the doors then manually relocked the front passenger door preventing passengers from even opening that door. I also had the front passenger seat moved way forward, I was hoping passengers would see the seat forward before they got in my car and take my hint – "*Sit in the back please?*"

I always crack my front windows prior to the pick-up location because some passengers will say something before they get in. When a passenger tried to open the locked front passenger door it was easy to politely request: *"Please ride in the back."*

I also had a sign displayed on my dash that explained that parties less than three are requested to ride in the back seat.

I put up the sign because I did not want anyone to think I was singling them out, my "please ride in the backseat policy" was true for everyone.

When passengers asked why I had them sit in the backseat I tried a variety of responses, most often simply pointing out that it was safer for everyone if passengers rode in the back. I did not enjoy these conversations.

If you think about it, having a passenger, a stranger, riding in your front seat when rideshare driving is an unnecessary distraction.

If nothing else I always feel a little uncomfortable looking in that direction while driving; my smart phone is mounted on the center of the dash and with a stranger in the front seat, especially if it's a woman, I'm worried they will think I'm looking at them when I'm looking at my phone.

When rideshare driving I am always at least a little uncomfortable with a stranger sitting in the front seat.

Some passengers can't stop themselves looking both ways for oncoming traffic, as if they were driving the car, an annoying habit.

Sometimes a passenger in the front seat will even lean forward blocking my ability to see and navigate safely.

Having passengers in the back does not seem to limit conversations, I have lots of great conversations with passengers in the backseat.

The primary reason I spent months forcing passengers to ride in the back seat, I was concerned my next passenger might be a "bad" one. If I did get a misbehaving passenger they would be easier to deal with if they were riding in the backseat.

Clearly, I did not have "My mind right" expecting the next passenger could be a "bad" one.

My focus could have been on the reality that most rideshare passengers behave respectfully. I was worrying that the next passenger would be one of the tiny percentage who do not behave in a respectful manner.

Think about this for a second:

> When I change my behavior as a rideshare driver, in anticipation something will go "wrong" with my next ride, I'm not behaving rationally, statistically 99% of rides and passengers will be "easy."

> **This is a clear example of me not having "My Mind Right."**

After at least a couple of months of having passengers sit in the back seat I got over it (got over myself?) I decided forcing passengers to sit in the back wasn't worth the trouble.

I didn't like the way the conversations were going when the conversation started with me explaining why I was doing something that most drivers were not doing.

If a passenger is only going to be in my car for a short time I prefer not spending any of that that time explaining my actions as the rideshare driver.

When I drive now I appreciate it when a passenger asks: *"Do you mind if I sit in the front?"*

I always respond: *"Wherever you are most comfortable."*

I'm not exactly lying but not telling the whole truth either.

I don't tell the whole truth because I don't want to have the conversation and not because I'm worried a passenger will only give me a four-star rating for asking them to ride in the back.

As a rideshare driver I exert control of the way my rides go by the actions I take as a rideshare driver, and also by the actions I do not take.

I choose to not make riding in the front seat an issue.

I read an article recently suggesting it is unlikely rideshare drivers will answer some passenger questions honestly, the article said rideshare drivers won't always give honest answers because they are concerned about getting a lower star rating from passengers.

When I answer questions, I'm not thinking about my star rating... I'm thinking about the kind of conversations I want to have during my day.

IS IT YOUR JOB TO "TRAIN" RIDESHARE PASSENGERS?

I realized early on that there is no reason to "train" rideshare passengers for their future rides for example by telling them how:

> To do a better job with the pick-up; find a safe place for a driver pick them up; to respond to the TNC application prompt to confirm where they are located

> To be at the pick-up location in a timely manner

> How they should behave in a rideshare driver's car

> That it is safer for everyone if they ride in the backseat

I don't believe it is a rideshare driver's "job" to "train" passengers in part because it is unlikely I will ever see them again; but primarily because **it would not be logical to create an uncomfortable environment between me and my passengers during a trip...** remember you are a business owner not an employee of the TNCs.

Here are a few examples:

- Sometimes the passenger pick-up will be less-than-smooth for any number of reasons including the passenger not being exactly where the map location pin drop shows them on the TNC's driver application map. My belief, I sometimes express out loud, is: *"We are together now so it's all good let's go."*

- Sometimes the first thing a passenger will say is: "We were watching you on the application map go to the wrong location."

  Typically, I don't acknowledge the comment with a response, instead I confirm the passenger name and the drop-off Location on the Trip Request and start driving.

  This is what I do when I have my "Mind Right." Instead of responding to a comment that bugged me I don't respond.

  Also, I try to not hold the comment against the passenger, likely they aren't trying to be disrespectful or rude, they were just making conversation.

- If the passenger's pick-up location is difficult because stationing my car at the exact pick-up location requires me to block traffic, I find a close and safe place to pull out of traffic.

    I will then call or text the passenger to make sure they know where to look for my car.

    Sometimes in these situations I have to circle the block, so I call the passenger, tell them there is no safe place to stop for the pick-up, ask if they will be available when I get back to their pick-up location.

    When I get the passenger in my car I don't tell them they could choose a better or safer pick-up location although sometimes I do say: *"Sorry you had to walk to me, but I could get a ticket for blocking traffic."*

    Notice I did not say anything about safety, no one wants to be told they created an unsafe situation especially when the did.

- I also keep my communications short and to the point anytime I am saying "No."

    Passengers don't want to hear "no" and most people who need to be told "no" are only going to react as if your "no" is part of a negotiating process and if they have the "right" responses they will get what they want.

As example when my next passenger calls me before the pick-up, and after talking to the passenger I decide for whatever reason I will not be continuing to their pick-up location.

When this happens, I go against my basic nature and hang up the phone as soon as I decide I will not be picking them up. I hang up without saying anything, not even "Goodbye."

I just don't see it as my responsibility to "train" passengers how to behave with a rideshare driver and

35

after I decide I will not be picking them up there is nothing to discuss.

After hanging up I choose "Cancel/No Charge" in the rideshare driving application, no charge means no transaction and no transaction in the TNC application means the passenger cannot give me a star rating or even easily contact the TNC to complain about my behavior.

- **Expanding on the last point,** I don't like hanging up on people, but I'm not going to say to someone:

  "I'm not going to pick you up because you sound like you are very drunk…"

  "I'm not going to pick you up because you obviously have no idea how to accurately describe where you are located, how in the heck do you expect me to find you?"

  "I'm not going to pick you up because you are being rude to me on the phone and I expect you will also behave in a less than respectful manner after you get in my car."

My norm is to not tell the passenger anything I think they did wrong, they don't want to hear it and I don't want to have the conversation.

If I try to "train" passengers for their future rideshare trips, it may sound to them like I'm scolding them or telling them they are wrong; I don't want an uncomfortable feeling with my passengers while I'm completing a trip.

My focus is always on earning income everything else is secondary.

USING THE "CANCEL/NO CHARGE" TNC APPLICATION OPTION

Author's Note: When I gave myself permission to use "Cancel/No Charge" feature I felt empowered. After spending months picking up passengers who weren't doing their part to insure smooth pick-ups, and sometimes making me feel disrespected on the phone or after they were in my car, I probably overused the "Cancel/No Charge" feature... for at least a few weeks. Now I use "Cancel/No Charge" sparingly but having this "power" continues to make my rideshare driving shifts more enjoyable and reduces my frustrations with the "job."

When a rideshare driver chooses to "Start trip" in the driver application it creates a transaction record in the TNC driver application and the TNC passenger application which makes it relatively easy for a rideshare passenger to write a complaint about you.

On any trip where the rideshare driver has selected "Start trip" the passenger will also have the option to give you a star rating.

If you never "Start trip" instead use the "Cancel/No Charge" feature, then there is no TNC financial transaction and the rideshare passenger will not be able to give you a star rating.

The passenger will have to work harder to contact the TNC to tell half-truths about a rideshare driver's actions... basically passengers unhappy because I did not pick them up.

These passengers will attempt to have the TNC believe it was the rideshare driver's fault they were not picked up or received a "No Show Cancellation Fee."

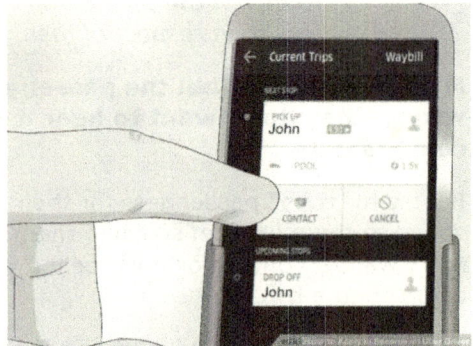

Thankfully a "No Show Cancellation Fee" is easy to verify, the TNC support organization can look at a driver's trip history and GPS location and will be able to see the car was at the passenger's pick-up location for the required amount of time and they will not reverse the "No Show Cancelation Fee."

I only choose "Cancel/No Show" option when I believe the passenger had every opportunity to get in my car on time.

Additionally, once a driver chooses the "Start trip" option they cannot immediately cancel the trip. The TNC application will say words to the effect of: "You have not traveled far enough to cancel this trip."

With Uber it is not possible to see the drop-off location until the rideshare driver selects "Start Trip." Making it difficult to cancel a trip makes it more difficult for Uber drivers to use "Start trip" to see the drop-off location then "Cancel/No Charge" before the passengers reach their car.

With Lyft it is possible to know the drop-off location after selecting "Confirm Arrival."

As an example of why I am suggesting you never "Start trip" until you are certain you agree to complete the trip, imagine three people come out of a private home, you confirm the name on the Trip Request they get into your backset saying someone else is coming... so you choose "Start trip."

Then two additional people come out of the house adding up to more passengers than you can legally transport in your car. You can still refuse to transport the passengers, but since you have already chosen "Start Trip" you will not be able to "Cancel/No Charge" or "Cancel/No Show" options, you will have to contact the TNC's support organization to communicate there was not a completed trip.

My goal is to never "Start trip" until I'm certain I have the right passengers in the car and I'm ready to drive away from the pick-up location and complete the trip.

I will sometimes use the option to "Cancel/No Charge" when:

1. Passengers take more than the allotted time to get into my car and I don't want to wait long enough to receive a Cancelation No Show payment.

   The passenger might stay inside their pick-up location (a bar, restaurant, home or apartment complex) until I have arrived; sent my arrival text message (Uber) or choose "Confirm Arrival" (Lyft); and waited long enough to warrant calling them on the phone: *"Hello this is your driver I'm at your pick-up location."*

   After talking to them on the phone they should appear almost immediately, getting a call from the rideshare driver is not the time to put on your shoes and start searching for your keys, wallet, purse, phone, etc.

   If I do wait for them the passenger will almost always say: *"Thanks for waiting"* but insincere apologies do not pay my bills. The TNCs communicate to passengers: "Be ready to go before you request a trip."

If every passenger kept me waiting 5 minutes, at the end of an 8-hour day I could have spent up to 2 hours waiting for late-arriving passengers and not earning income.

This is also means that only 2-3 long waits at pick-up locations during an 8-hour day could mean I've completed 1 or 2 less trips during that rideshare driving shift. If I lose 1 to 2 trips per day at the end of a week I could be looking at $50-$100 less income or $200 to $400 less in a month of full-time driving.

As a rideshare driver time is money and long waits at the pick-up location cost potential income.

Every driver will have to find their own comfort level for waiting at the pick-up locations and calling passengers. There is certainly a case suggesting rideshare drivers should call every passenger immediately, or maybe 30 seconds or so after arriving at the pick-up location.

2. Passengers who have clearly ignored the TNC application prompt to "Confirm your pick-up location" and are in a very different location, a location where they would not be able to see my car sitting at the pick-up location indicated on the TNC application map.

   When I talk to this kind of potential passenger on the phone they typically say: *"I'm outside looking for you, where are you?"*

   Typically, I will say: *"I'm at your pick-up location as indicated on the Uber application map."* When I've said this, most passengers respond as if they have no idea what I am talking about.

   These passengers seem to expect me to spend minutes on the phone and driving around trying to find them, as if this process was somehow part of the rideshare driving experience. I'm sorry (not really), I don't agree 2-5 minutes of attempting to find passengers at pick-up locations is part of the rideshare transportation experience.

Once I spent at least five minutes talking to a passenger on the phone, he kept saying: "*I think I see you now*" so I did not hang up and cancel the ride.

We were in downtown Denver and there were a lot of people on the streets and a lot of Uber/Lyft cars picking up passengers.

After about five minutes on the phone he asked: "*Are you on Arapahoe?*"

I responded: "*No I'm on Lawrence, at the pick-up location shown on the Uber map.*"

When this passenger got in my car he said: "*Sorry but I guess Uber didn't accurately identify my pick-up location.*"

I did not respond: "*It's not Uber's fault that you ignored the prompt to confirm your location on the Uber passenger application map; and it's not Uber's fault that when we talked on the phone you did not immediately tell me you were on Arapahoe.*"

Sometimes passengers cannot accurately describe where they are or sometimes they are a significant distance away from their pin-drop on the TNC application map.

It is very common for passengers to ask on the phone: "*Where are you*" instead of attempting to communicate where they are located.

An appropriate (however rude) response to the potential passenger's question: "*Where are you?*"

Would be: "*I'm located in a car with wheels and a motor and you are located somewhere with only your feet to get around, wouldn't it make more sense for you to at least try to tell me where you are? If I knew where you were I could drive my car to you?*"

Of course, I would never say that to a potential passenger, if I was done with them I would simply hang up the phone and choose: "Cancel/No Charge."

After overusing the "Cancel/No Charge" feature for a few weeks I relaxed a bit and realized a completed trip means more income, also true, a completed trip will produce more income than a "No Show Cancellation Fee"; but sometimes I still make the choice to "Cancel/No Charge" in order to protect my peace of mind.

MORE ON THE PASSENGER PICK-UP

When I arrive at any Uber pick-up Location (as shown on the Uber driver application map) I send a text message:

> *"UBER--- At your map location pin drop... Silver Toyota Prius look for YELLOW LIGHTBULB on antenna."*

In the past two years I have revised my Uber arrival text wording many times, after some great tips from a passenger I settled on this one and have been using it for over a year.

The intent of my Uber arrival text is three-fold:

1. Mark the moment I arrived at the pick-up location, so I know exactly when the trip is eligible for a "Cancel/No Show" fee.

2. To help the passenger find me, "silver Toyota Prius" and "Yellow light bulb on antenna."

3. To remind passengers it's time to go.

With Lyft pick-ups I don't send a text message when I arrive at the pick-up location. When I arrive for a Lyft pick-up there is a "Confirm Arrival" option which sends the equivalent of a text message to the Lyft passenger, the passenger's phone makes a distinctive tone.

If I've been waiting more than a few minutes for a Lyft passenger I will call them on the phone, but it rarely happens with Lyft passengers. I don't think Lyft passengers are on average better at getting to the car, I think the Lyft application does a better job of notifying passengers that their car is waiting.

At rideshare driver events I have heard some drivers say they always call their passengers as soon as they arrive at the pick-up location. Some of my passengers have told me they wouldn't mind a phone call when the rideshare driver arrives at pick-up location; these passengers say they would consider a phone call good customer service.

I've thought about calling passengers when I arrive at the pick-up location, but I've learned from experience if I'm doing something most drivers are not doing it can result in conversations I don't want to have. I'm also not willing to "train" passengers for their future rides.

On the other hand, long waits at the pick-up add up and cost me income.

Also true, if a passenger is located somewhere other than the pick-up location indicated on the TNC application map it is better to know sooner than later.

If you choose to give rideshare driving "a go" you will have to decide how you behave, you are "the boss." Most passengers are in the car soon after you arrive at their pick-up location without adding an extra step of calling.

Important note on using the "Cancel/No Show" option: After I've charged a passenger a "Cancel/No Show" fee I don't want to be called back to the pick-up location for the same passenger.

If they were just charged a cancellation fee they are probably going to want to have a conversation about why I marked them as a: "No Show."

That conversation is probably going to feel like the passenger thinks I did something wrong. The passenger may blame the TNC application or make some other excuse for not being available to be picked up and ask me to get the cancellation fee reversed.

I'm not willing to make judgement calls, these passengers could be lying or exaggerating the truth trying to get their way. I prefer to prevent the conversations from happening.

Downing St

700 ft

Kingman Estates Winery
800 E 64th Ave, Denver, CO

1 min
E 64th Ave

62nd Ave

iBAKE Denver

▲ NAVIGATE

🔔 Rider notified

Sheldon · Pickup

Some people seem to enjoy arguing with a cashier, a waiter, a bartender, a manager, a rideshare driver, etc. trying to save a few dollars and this is not a conversation I want to have when I am "trapped" with a stranger riding in my car.

To prevent this scenario I will sometimes go offline for 5 minutes or so allowing time for the cancelled passenger to get a ride from another driver. Since I drive for Uber and Lyft I am still available for a Trip Request with one TNC application offline.

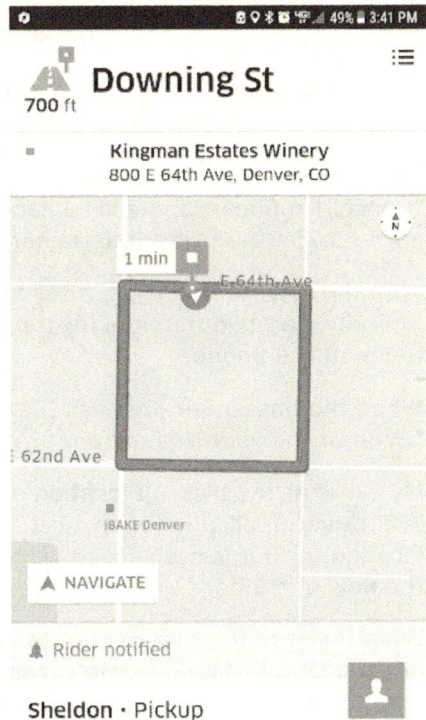

Alternatively, I don't go offline I just make sure I remember the passenger name on the "Cancel/No Show" trip so if I get an immediate Trip Request and it's the same passenger name I won't go back to pick-up someone who was just charged a cancellation fee.

"CANCEL/NO CHARGE" AND "START TRIP" - Part Two

There are two basic types of rides, private and shared.

With a "private ride trip" the passenger has five minutes to be in your car from the moment you arrive at the pick-up location.

With the less-expensive "shared ride" trips, passengers have two minutes to be in the car.

If passengers exceed the time limits the driver can choose the option to "Cancel/No Show" and earn a cancellation fee, in early 2018 drivers earn $3.75 for an Uber passenger no show and $5 for a Lyft no show.

With the private ride trips, after arriving at the pick-up location, I typically wait two minutes for the passenger to be in my car then I call them on the phone.

When the passenger answers the phone I always say the same thing: "*Hello this is your driver I am at your location.*"

My car is at the pick-up location as indicated by the pin drop on the TNC driver application map. If I have any question about the pin drop location, or if it is not safe to wait at the pin drop (get my car out of the flow of traffic) I will call as soon as I arrive.

When I call at the two-minute mark the passengers are, in my opinion, already late getting into the car even though technically they still have another three minutes before I can choose "Cancel/No Show" and earn a cancelation fee.

When a passenger requests a trip, they should be ready to go, the TNC passenger applications communicate this to passengers "Do not request a trip until you are ready to go":

- After a driver accepts the Trip Request, TNC passenger application communicates expected wait time: "Your driver will arrive in approximately 5 minutes."

- Progress of the approaching rideshare ride is displayed on the TNC passenger application map, a moving icon displayed on the TNC passenger application map shows exactly where the car is currently located at the icon moves as the driver's car approaches the pick-up location.

- When the driver arrives the TNC passenger application alerts them with a tone and a message: "Your driver has arrived."

Consider this: If passengers were ready to go when they requested the ride, getting to the car in two minutes or less should be easy. In the example above, the passenger has an additional 5 minutes to be ready to go.

Sometimes I am traveling 10 minutes or more to get to a passenger's pick-up location, if the passenger keeps me waiting more than two minutes after I have traveled 10 minutes to get them, hard to argue that is not rude behavior on the passenger's part. They have had over twelve minutes to be ready to go.

When the passenger answers the phone I immediately say: *"Hello this is your driver, I am at your location."*

Straight to the point because I don't want to waste more of my time in a cumbersome phone conversation, I'm not an old friend calling to catch up, the passenger is late getting into my car and I'm trying to maximize my earnings, most of my income comes from mileage not from the smaller payment I receive for my time waiting.

When it is immediately obvious the passenger didn't bother to confirm their pick-up location on the TNC passenger application map, (passengers are prompted by the Uber and Lyft passenger applications to "Confirm Pick-up Location" see graphic to the right) and it's obvious in the phone conversation the passenger expects me to spend more than a few seconds of my time finding them at a different location, I'm probably going hang up without even saying "goodbye" and use the "Cancel/No Charge" option.

This might be the one exception where I am willing to "train" passengers for future rides, passengers should be confirming their pick-up locations, and if they are not at the pick-up location indicated on the TNC passenger

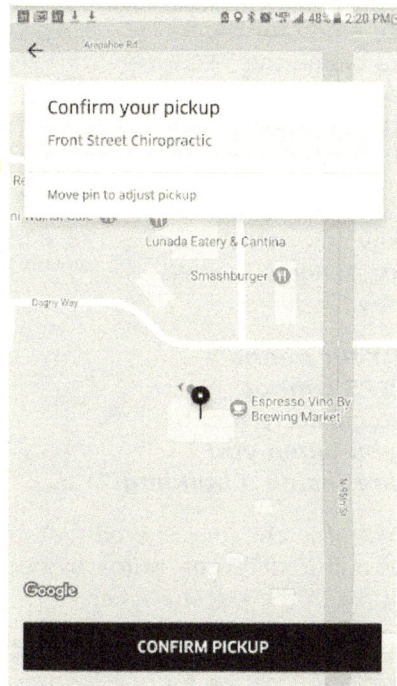

Confirm your pickup

Front Street Chiropractic

Move pin to adjust pickup

Lunada Eatery & Cantina

Smashburger

Dagny Way

Espresso Vino By Brewing Market

Google

CONFIRM PICKUP

application they really should not be rewarded with a ride, they should be penalized with a no-show cancelation fee.

I have spent considerable time thinking about making this passenger "training" exception. It is my hope word will spread that part of the rideshare driving experience is figuring out how to accurately display your location in the TNC passenger application. If you don't have the correct location in the TNC passenger application you may not get picked up by the first driver who accepts your Trip Request, and you may get charged a $5 no show cancellation fee.

In other words, I'm training passengers by not picking them up.

Passengers have the option to confirm or update the pick-up location in the TNC passenger application, but some passengers seem to assume their phone's GPS reading and the TNC application will somehow always get their pick-up location correct, "Like Magic", in my experience: "Not so much."

In fact, when a passenger who was not at their pin-drop location gets in my car it's common for them to blame the TNC application for getting their location wrong.

If I were willing to say spicy things to passengers I would say:

"Your phone's GPS cannot accurately locate you when you are inside a building!"

GPS works great in America when the smart phone's GPS is communicating with four or more GPS satellites.

Since GPS requires line of sight to the sky the phone's GPS can see exactly zero satellites while inside a building.

When the TNC application requests a GPS reading it gets the last known GPS location which could be anywhere, the GPS reading reports where the phone was the last time it updated it's GPS location.

Locations are also tracked by WiFi and cell tower signals but these readings do not have the accuracy of a GPS communicating with four or more satellites.

In 7,000+ trips I have never explained GPS to a passenger because I do not train passengers for their future rides.

With the cheaper Shared Ride trips my pick-up location arrival process is a little different, primarily because passengers have only two minutes to be in the rideshare car.

If I don't already have a shared ride passenger in my car, I wait at the pick-up location for one minute then I call and use my standard greeting as soon as they answer their phone: "*Hello this is your driver I am at your location.*"

With the shared ride trips, when I already have passengers in my car, I call as soon as I arrive at pick-up location. I won't wait the full two minutes, or even one minute; with passengers already in my car I take immediate action hoping to pick-up the new passenger quickly and continue with the ride.

I usually take the effort to call private and shared ride passengers because completing a trip and earning a fare is almost always more income than a cancellation fee.

When I was a new driver I was more likely to sit and wait for the full five or two minutes before taking action. After months of driving I decided the TNC's wait time metric should only be for worst-case scenarios.

I never want to be late to any engagement but sometimes I mess up and arrive late, everyone can mess up occasionally but if most of your passengers are keeping you waiting, statistically-speaking it's more likely passengers think it's ok to use most of the allotted wait time before they could be charged a cancellation fee.

When I first started driving it seemed like every trip with CU Boulder college student passengers kept me waiting at least a few minutes at the curb. The rides in Boulder are usually short, Minimum Fares, add in the long wait times and it's no wonder my earnings were significantly lower compared to driving in Denver where trips are longer, and passengers are less likely to keep drivers waiting at the curb.

When passengers get in the car "late," I won't say anything about waiting too long, because I'm not in the business of training rideshare passengers and I don't want to have any uncomfortable conversations as part of my work day.

If the passenger says: "*Sorry to keep you waiting.*" I typically respond: "*No worries, we're together now let's go!*"

Agreed, I'm not being honest but really what would be the point of saying anything else?

I always want to be treated with respect. Passengers who wait until the rideshare driver calls them on the phone, then expect the rideshare driver to spend additional time finding them (probably because they didn't bother to confirm their pick-up location) are not being respectful.

Unfortunately, since about two-thirds of rideshare drivers have less than three months on the road these passengers probably have been picked up by "rookie" drivers even though keeping drivers waiting at the curb is disrespectful (and frankly lazy) behavior.

Getting picked up without doing their "job" as a rideshare passenger, teaches rideshare passengers that it is ok to not do their part to insure smooth pick-ups.

MORE ON SHARED TRIPS – LYFT SHARED & UBER POOL

The two dominate TNCs in Denver/Boulder offer a discount to rideshare passengers if they agree to share their ride with other passengers traveling on more-or-less the same route. This TNC transportation option is more accurately "rideshare" compared to a private ride trip which is more like a traditional taxi ride.

The price difference offered to the passenger, at least for short trips, is usually not significantly less than a private trip, but one passenger told me on a medium length trip he was offered $18 or $9 for the trip... a discount hard for anyone to turn down.

After hearing $9 or $18 for the trip, I asked a few shared trip passengers if they remembered the price difference, shared vs. private, but pretty quickly decided I didn't care enough to have conversations on that topic be part of my work day.

With the shared ride trips, drivers are paid the same amounts for mileage and travel time, but with each new passenger there is an additional pick-up, making the shared ride trips feel like more work for the rideshare driver.

There will also be addition wait times and wait time income is less mileage income. Rideshare driver earnings are primarily from how many miles driven with paying passengers, not wait time payments, in the rideshare driving gig, time really is money.

In late 2017 Uber added an additional small payment to the driver for each new passenger, less than a dollar for each additional passenger, but in my experience the shared ride option almost always feels like more work for essentially the same income.

On the other hand, shared trips are often medium to long trips... think about the $18 or $9 example, saving a dollar on a short trip is not as tempting as saving a lot on a medium to long trip.

Once you accept the first shared ride trip, additional passengers are added to your passenger queue automatically. This is true with Uber and Lyft shared ride trips. You are not presented with new Trip Requests you can choose to accept/reject or just let go by without a response.

It is still possible to reject the additional Trip Requests, but you will have to use the "Cancel/No Charge" option to remove them from your passenger Queue.

You will have to "play" with the TNC driver application to find the option to "Cancel/No Charge" a specific passenger, read carefully, you don't want to cancel the whole ride, just the passenger you do not plan to pick-up.

You can stop getting any new Trip Requests by turning on the feature that says you will complete current trips but do not want additional Trip Requests or additional shared ride passengers. Sometimes I will do this if for no other reason to take a breath, have an empty car for a moment, then go immediately back online.

The TNC's have different rules for the share ride trips compared to rules for private passenger trips.

Shared Ride rules typically include:

- Not deviating from the route on the GPS navigation application

- Not making additional stops, no stops at the gas station to pick up a pack of smokes

- Not changing the passenger drop-off location, the TNC application will not let drivers or passengers change the drop-off location in the application

Bear in mind the TNCs are expecting rideshare drivers to enforce the shared ride rules but the TNCs cannot require independent contractor drivers to enforce share ride rules or even explain the shared ride rules.

I make judgement calls, if we don't have other passengers in the car or waiting to be picked-up, and the shared ride passenger askes respectfully to run into the gas station for a pack of smokes, I will usually say "Yes."

I don't like the conversations that can happen when a shared ride passenger is trying to get me to bend or break the shared ride rules; however, I will never speak as if I'm an employee of Uber or Lyft when talking about the shared ride rules.

I might say something like:

"Since you chose the cheaper shared ride and we have other passengers to consider I can't make changes to the trip."

I will never say: *"With Uber Pool you cannot get a stop at the gas station for a pack of smokes."*

Again, I suggest you not train passengers for their future trips, it makes no sense to make these conversations part of your work day.

For a long time, I did not like the shared ride trips, but recently, I'm warming up to them.

Sometimes the TNC application software does not find a matching passenger making a shared ride trip exactly like a private ride trip; however, shared ride trips can still "feel" significantly different than the private ride trip because:

- Some passengers will ask you to break the rules of the share ride option by asking you to stop at a store or take a different navigation route or change their drop-off location.

  When this happens the TNC's hope you, the rideshare driver, will enforce the share trip rules and say "No."

  The TNCs also hope the rideshare driver will explain why they said "no."

However, the TNCs cannot tell independent contractor drivers how to safely transport passengers from Point A to Point B and I'm not willing to have conversations I would prefer not to have with my passengers.

- Shared ride trip mixes strangers in your car. If for example, some passengers have been drinking alcohol and others have not, the trip can feel awkward for the rideshare driver. I didn't sign up to rideshare drive thinking I would be arbitrating conflicts with mixed groups of strangers traveling in my car.

- With private ride trips there is a natural break between trips even when you have already accepted your next Trip Request.

  With shared ride trips passengers can be in and out of your car without a break in the action - the natural breaks don't exist.

  Recently I had several back-to-back shared ride trips with passengers in and out of my car for almost two hours.

  It felt like more than two hours because many of the passengers were being "spicy" expecting spirited but respectful conversations with the driver, me.

  I usually don't mind respectful, but "spicy" passengers; but with shared ride trips passengers who are not calm and relatively quiet can add to the often-exhausting feeling of completing shared ride trips.

  > Once with a Shared Trip Passenger already in my car I was assigned a new Passenger so made a turn headed for the new Pickup. After about a minute the new Passenger canceled and the GPS directed me to turn back toward the previous route. Then another new passenger was added the GPS directed me to again make a quick turn in a different direction. This happened during rush hour traffic and I chose to reduce my stress my canceling the new Passenger and telling the TNC Application I needed a break. Once I dropped of the original passenger I went immediately back online.

- The experience of completing shared ride trips can be overwhelming when lots of things are happening at the same time: when passengers are chatty, for example asking you a bunch of questions about being a rideshare driver; you are getting assigned additional trips; your music is playing; traffic is heavy; a new passenger is automatically added and your GPS navigation route suddenly changes expecting you to cross multiple lanes of traffic to make an almost immediate turn, remember be safe, if you can't safely make the turn the world will not come to an end because it took you a little longer to get to the new pick-up location.

- While I'm always more interested in a completed trip compared to a cancellation fee, I am more likely to "Cancel/No Show" shared ride trips if the passenger takes more than two minutes to get into my car, even when I don't have shared ride passenger already in the car.

  With shared ride trips the passengers are supposed to be, more-or-less, at the curb waiting for the rideshare driver to arrive.

  I think not being at the car in two minutes or less is extremely disrespectful of the rideshare driver, other passengers in the shared ride trip, and the discounted fare offer from the TNC.

  The ride is cheaper because the TNCs are expecting the passenger to do their part to insure everyone is making the best use of their time.

- Shared ride passengers will sometimes "play dumb" and say they didn't realize they had requested the shared ride option.

  When this happens, I say something like: "If you are presented with two options and choose the lower price you are choosing the shared ride" then I shut up.

  These passengers may be hoping you treat the trip like a private ride and not pick up additional passengers and they may have been successful in the past, remember two-thirds of rideshare drivers have been on the road less than 90 days and it is easier to take advantage of a new drivers, especially new drivers who have bought into the idea that rideshare drivers should always be eager to please rideshare passengers.

When shared ride trips first launched in Denver it was common to hear passengers complain to drivers when a new passenger pick-up was added to their trip:

Passengers saying: *"What? I didn't choose to share my ride with other passengers!"*

The TNCs released updated online trainings and send email and in-application notifications explaining that every driver should see the new training session on shared ride trips.

The training showed drivers exactly what passengers were seeing in the TNC passenger application when they booked a shared ride trip, convinced me more than a few passengers were lying to me. Before I saw the online trainings, I wondered if the TNC passenger application was clearly explaining the shared ride rules.

The TNC online training session proved the rules for shared ride trips are explained to passengers very clearly. I believe that if the passengers aren't paying attention it's not my job as the rideshare driver to accommodate them, next time they can pay attention.

Important note, and I'm repeating myself, I will not say anything to knowingly create an uncomfortable conversation in my car... I'm simply not going to do it.

As a full-time driver I am completing about 80 trips every week, my car, my office, I control the office environment.

- After two or more shared ride trips in a row, I sometimes turn on the feature that says I will complete the trips I have already been assigned but want to sign off after dropping off the last passenger already in my passenger queue.

  I might immediately go back online but sometimes I need a break in the sometimes, non-stop action of the shared ride experience.

KNOW WHEN TO SHUT UP?

It's common for most people to feel anxious with an "uncomfortable silence," especially when in close quarters with other people. This is especially true for me, and even after 11,000+ trips, I still sometimes think I should fill silence in my car with words... especially with passengers in the front passenger seat.

While I am naturally on edge at least a little when meeting new people, I also have "the gift of gab" so the ability to converse at least semi-intelligently on almost any topic and relate to a wide variety of people.

Also true, I sometimes have the tendency to "run my mouth" telling stories; sharing my thoughts on a given subject; and basically fill almost any silence with some kind of conversation.

Over time as a rideshare driver I've learned to become more comfortable with silence when I am transporting rideshare passengers.

If you choose to rideshare drive you will make your own rules, here are my basic rules, common practices, regarding my side of in-car conversations:

- After confirming I have the correct name on the Trip Request and the correct drop-off location I usually make a comment about the weather or some other generic topic which communicates my willingness to have conversations, then I let the rideshare passenger's response guide what happens next.

- If it seems a rideshare passenger is not holding up their end of the conversation, I have learned to let the conversation stop or even sometimes feel like it has gone "thud" and leave it at that.

  If a passenger wants to talk they will restart a conversation.

  If they don't restart a conversation, I typically do not feel stress remembering that it is unlikely they will leave a tip no matter what I do or more accurately if they are going to leave a tip how chatty I am will probably not be a factor.

  When conversation seems to have died off... I might turn up the volume on my music, just a little.

- While I believe I am an interesting person with stories to tell and valuable experiences to share... I have settled on the goal of getting the passengers to talk about what they want to talk about.

  I don't always succeed and sometimes I feel like I've been running my mouth, but my goal is always that my passengers talk more than I do.

At the end of some trips I have been known to say: "*Thank you for listening to me talk*" if I feel I have dominated the conversation. This not about my driver star rating, it is about me feeling good about how I conduct myself.

- To show I'm listening and to "draw in" my passengers I try to say things like: "*I agree with what you said when…*" and "*It's just like you said…*"

Everyone wants to feel heard and the conversations and trips go smoother when passengers feel heard.

I only say this when it is true, I don't want to sound disingenuous. Looking for points of agreement helps me be a better listener.

- I don't lie, exaggerate, or be purposefully misleading mostly because it's just not who I am.

When I started rideshare driving, a close friend pointed out that I could say pretty much anything because it is unlikely I will ever see the same passengers again after dropping them off.

Frankly I thought about having fun with my passengers thinking: "Where's the harm" but settled on the reality that I don't want to be lied to or mislead or hear stories with wild exaggeration so I'm not going to subject my passengers to the same.

- Some passengers will make it very clear they are not looking for conversation.

Often there will be subtle clues like one word and low-volume acknowledgements when I confirm the name on the Trip Request and the drop-off location or they immediately busy themselves on their smart phones.

I don't take this passenger behavior personally; seasoned rideshare passengers may not be interested in talking to every new rideshare driver.

- Remember your passengers are strangers and you don't know anything about them, their background, or what they might be feeling stress about, so don't assume everyone is having "a great day" and talk to them as if conversation was an expectation or requirement of the rideshare experience.

- When I have more than one passenger, I try to never insert myself into their conversations or if they are quiet I am quiet.

  I am always surprised when two or more people ride along in relative silence and it happens more often than you might think.

  It might help to remember that you have no idea what transpired before these passengers entered your car... they might be having a rough day or maybe it is a couple taking a pause from an ongoing fight and by trying to spark conversation you are going to sound like (and probably end up feeling like) a dork trying to "liven up" the trip with your witty repartee.

  Just respect the silence and drive.

- I don't care if passengers talk on their phones during their trip; after all my primary goal is making money and if they are on talking on their phone or are busy doing something with their phone so what?

  In fact, I see it as a bonus when passengers are on the phone or buried in a smart phone application because then I don't feel anxious because we're not having conversation.

  I treat passenger phone conversations the same way I treat conversations with multiple passengers in the same trip; I try to not make it clear that I have heard everything they have said by commenting on their private phone call.

  When a passenger is on the phone I turn down the music a little, I want them to be able to hear their call but also don't want them to feel I'm eavesdropping on their phone conversation.

  Again, I don't care if passengers talk on their phones because I know my primary goal is making money and everything else is secondary.

- Sometimes when I don't feel much like talking and I'll say something that might end conversation until the trip is completed.

  As example after confirming the rideshare passenger name and drop-off location I might say: *"Looks like about a 10-minute drive"* then I shut up and turn the music up a little as if that is what I do on every trip.

ADDITIONAL TRIP REQUESTS DURING AN ACTIVE TRIP

In my experience it is common to receive the next Trip Request from the TNC application during an active trip. This means I might complete two or more trips in a row for Lyft after accepting a Lyft Trip Request.

After completing an active trip, and the last passengers have exited my car, if I don't have a new active Trip Request to complete with the same TNC (or cancel without charging the passenger), then I'll go back to having both Uber and Lyft driver applications active.

Typically, when completing multiple trips in a row for the same TNC, the next pick-up location for the new trip will be a few minutes away from the last passenger's drop-off location.

If the new Trip Request doesn't make sense to me, maybe the pick-up location is 10-minute drive and I'm already in a high-traffic area, I can always choose "Cancel/No Charge" in the TNC driver application without traveling to the pick-up location.

By offering an additional Trip Request during the active trip, the TNC software has determined that even after dropping off your current passenger, you are the driver in the best position to arrive at the new passenger's pick-up location first.

You get another trip to complete and passengers get faster pick-ups - a win-win situation.

DRIVING IN A SPECIFIC AREA AND EARNING BEFORE AN APPOINTMENT

Sometimes my passengers ask me where I live, what part of the city, and are often surprised if I've picked them up more than a 30-minute drive from my home. Some people's mental image of rideshare driving doesn't match up with reality.

Where I drive, (Denver Colorado) it is common for me to be driving 30 minutes or more from where I live.

Some rideshare drivers live outside of large cities and commute to the city before going online to accept rides. Rideshare drivers who live in an area with a smaller population really don't have any choice, there won't be a lot of Trip Requests far away from population centers.

Another common passenger question is variations of: "What part of the city do you prefer to drive?"

My normal answer is: "*I go where the rides take me*" or "*I'm going where you are going.*" After we get on our way to the passenger's drop-off location, we will probably discuss the topic further.

It's possible passengers asking questions about where a driver lives or prefers to drive ask all their drivers the same questions.

Remember that about 2/3 of rideshare drivers have been on the road less than 90 days, the answers different drivers give to the most common passenger questions might be all over the map. I assume some passengers are just curious to hear the different answers?

The TNC applications do have a few ways to give drivers some control over where they drive; however, these features mean limiting Trip Requests, so likely means less Trip Requests.

Limiting the types of Trip Requests you receive may mean you are taking yourself off "the list" for longer, more profitable trips.

The Trip Request limiting feature I use most often is called Destination Mode – this feature allows me to enter a destination address, as example, my home address. In theory I will be offered only Trip Requests with a drop-off location on the way to my home address.

The Destination Mode feature usually works well, although sometimes it means receiving a Trip Request that requires 15 minutes or so to complete without moving me much closer to my destination address.

Sometimes, the Destination Mode feature will not find any Trip Requests on the way to my destination. It's worth trying, I have occasionally received long Trip Requests taking me on an almost direct path to my destination, so earned a nice fare and moved significantly closer to my target destination.

Using "basic" Destination Mode does not control what time you need to arrive at your destination. A TNC's Destination Mode feature may include a Destination Arrival Time setting which further controls what kind of Trip Requests you receive.

For example, with the Destination Mode Arrival Time setting I can enter the address of my children's school and 2:30pm for my arrival time, the time school lets out.

Using the arrival time feature might mean I get a Trip Request with a drop-off location in the opposite direction, but in theory I will always have enough time to arrive at my appointment on time.

As example, once, while located in downtown Denver, I set the Destination Mode address for home and arrival time for two hours from the present time. The first Trip Request I received took me over 30 minutes in the opposite direction from home. When the time came to start driving to my destination by the Arrival Time I entered, I was notified by the TNC driver application: "It's time to start driving toward your destination."

I made some nice fares that day using Destination Mode, also ended up driving over 30 minutes to my destination without a paying trip. Not a big deal, it's part of the rideshare driving gig.

I suggest every driver experiment with all the TNC driver application features, remembering that one or two experiences is probably not statistically significant, if you don't get any Trip Requests the first few times you use Destination Mode that doesn't mean the feature doesn't work, it just didn't work that day.

If you use Destination Mode before an important appointment pay attention, don't count completely on the TNC driver application which might have an error and send you a Trip Request you cannot complete without being late to the appointment.

Once using Destination Mode with an Arrival Time, from my current location my target destination required about 10 minutes driving, I received a Trip Request with a drop-off location almost 40 minutes away.

I did not know the drop-off location until I had the passengers and their luggage in my car, remember drivers do not know where passengers are going until choosing the "Start Trip" option.

I had to explain to the passengers I was using a TNC driver application feature that should have meant we were not matched for the trip. Without going into detail how Destination Mode works (passengers don't care) I explained I had an appointment in 30 minutes that was just a few minutes' drive from our current location.

I had to explain that I could not transport them because their destination was 40 minutes away and I would miss my appointment. I had to unload their luggage and tell them they would have to call another driver.

TNC application errors do happen and I assume this was one of them. Until that day I had never refused a trip based on the destination, an exception to my normal rule to complete almost every passenger trip I'm offered… it was not my fault but I still felt a little bad for the passengers.

In practice, when using Destination Mode with Arrival Time, I set my desired arrival time about 30 minutes prior to the actual appointment time, that way I'm not rushing to arrive on time and might even have time to stop for coffee.

Using basic Destination Mode (no Arrival Time) might send you a Trip Request that does not advance you toward your destination.

One night I was using the Destination Feature configured with my home address and received a Trip Request requiring me to exit the highway and complete a Minimum Fare trip. Completing the trip took about 20 minutes and I earned Minimum Fare income, about $3.40 and the passenger's drop-off location, if anything, left me a bit farther from home.

I opened a support ticket requesting an explanation why the Destination Mode feature sent me a Trip Request that did not advance me towards my configured destination. The support team's response was basically: "This can happen." The trip didn't take me very far off my route, but it didn't get me any closer to my destination either.

The Destination Mode feature has increased my income. Before Destination Mode, the three days I pick my children up at school, I lost about an hour each day of potential earning time.

Before Destination Mode I went offline about an hour and a half before school let out. With Destination Mode and Arrival Time I gained about an hour of additional work time every day I pick up my children from school.

Thanks to the Destination Mode feature I gained about three hours earning time every week, the additional income is about $50 dollars per week or about $200 additional earnings every month.

The Destination Mode feature also helped plan my rideshare driving days when I have a doctor's appointment. If the appointment time is in the middle of a block of time I plan to drive I can use Destination Mode to increase my time online earning income.

Destination Mode was an important value-add from Uber and Lyft increasing my income.

Rideshare driving is still relatively new and the TNCs are doing what they can to improve their services for drivers and passengers. Because of the high attrition rate for new drivers, and the shortage of available drivers, it is logical to assume Uber, Lyft, Taxify, and the other TNCs will continue to add features that benefit drivers hoping to attract and retain available rideshare drivers to use the TNC's driver applications.

Having the TNC's essentially fighting over available drivers is certainly a good thing.

When you are attempting to limit the type of trips you complete, remember, how you choose to do the job is up to you, "Your ride, your rules" and when you are trying to control where you drive you can always choose to refuse a trip at the pick-up location.

If you refuse a trip because you are trying to control where you drive, it would be polite to explain your reason to the passenger you are refusing to transport: *"I don't have time to complete your trip before I have to pick up my children at school."*

It is always my goal to treat others the way I want to be treated, so I do everything I can to avoid refusing rides except when passengers show with their behavior they do not belong in my car, like my Ice Cream Cone Man experience. (explained later)

Some TNC driver applications will have other features for limiting Trip Requests, such as the ability to limit the part of the city a driver works, I have never used them.

When I'm driving my goal is always maximizing my earnings, and I don't want to miss a long trip because I'm trying to contain my rides to a particular part of town.

I use Destination Mode primarily on school days and when I'm going home at the end of a day/shift of driving. Most of the time I am working, I have the TNC driver application in its' default mode, open to all trips.

If I am feeling tired and/or feeling like I want to go home, sometimes I just go offline and drive home. I know my earnings average out over time and one more trip is not going to "make or break" my rideshare business.

It often feels nice to spontaneously decide I am done for the day, go offline, I'm done. I enjoy the control and the freedom.

Deciding when to work is part of being an independent contractor. Sometimes it can be tempting to stay out longer than your plan, perhaps you see Surge Pricing displayed on the TNC driver application map and think it would be nice to "cash in" on higher fares.

Alternatively, you may have trouble motivating yourself to get on the road and earn. This is the nature of the rideshare driving gig, the nature of working for yourself, the nature of being an independent contractor, your own boss.

More than once I've thought: *"One more trip then I'm going home,"* without using Destination Mode and then the "one more trip" drop-off location was over 30 minutes in the opposite direction from my home.

A few times when I'm thinking: *"I'll complete one or two more trips then go home"* and I've gotten a really long ride, an hour or more driving, a nice fare but if I was thinking about going home because I was tired… it is not cool or safe to be fighting sleep while you are driving.

In conclusion, remember you are an independent contractor doing gig work. Running Uber and Lyft applications simultaneously can lead to stressful situations if you react to the situation with stress.

Also remember the linear nature of rideshare driving, you can only complete a finite number of trips per hour, when I drive I'm usually thinking more trips means more money so I don't "Cancel/No Charge" trips unless I believe it makes sense.

Breathe and relax, do what you need to do and stay focused on your primary goal – making money. And be safe on the road, don't break the cardinal rule: "First do no harm."

YOUR RIDESHARE DRIVING OFFICE ESSENTIALS

One of the ways I approach rideshare driving in a professional manner, making sure I always have the essentials available in my office (my car) before I head out to drive.

With every job I've ever had I had a process for getting myself ready to go to work: when I worked in IT I needed my laptop, cell phone, etc.; when I was a waiter I needed to remember to bring my apron and pens; and as a rideshare driver I have a process, a plan, how to get ready to get on the road and earn.

Some items in my office (car) I consider essential, and some are just nice to have:

- **Things I consider essential:**

    o   A charger and dash mount for my phone

    o   Commercial-free music, I don't play the radio in part because I don't want to play commercials to my passengers and because I want to control the music I listen to for hours at a time.

    o   A full tank of gas, at least mostly full, I don't want to get a nice long trip and be forced to stop for gas on the way. Also, gas in some parts of Denver/Boulder can be $0.50 a gallon more than my local station.

    o   Kleenex, or at least a stack of fast-food napkins (for me and my passengers.) Passengers will sometimes ask for a tissue, and when I have a box of tissues I have offered to passengers who sounded like they needed them.

    o   Air freshener (for the car) I rarely use the air freshener but always have a can in the glove box. I don't like heavy smells, so I use an air freshener made from citrus fruits, when I spray a tiny bit it smells like someone peeled an orange in my car.

o   One-gallon zip-lock "car sick" bags (for my passengers and my peace-of-mind)

I have two bags tucked in the seatback pockets and I've labeled the tops "Just in case" using a label maker.

Since I started driving, the rare times when I have someone at risk for throwing up in my car, I give the passenger a bag and the passenger almost always said: *"I'm not going to get sick in your car"* and I respond: *"That's ok, the bag is just in case."*

It's common for my passengers to comment on the "Just in case" label and ask about passengers throwing up. They think my "Just in case" bags are funny and a good idea.

I like the idea that seeing the bags gives passenger a picture of rideshare driving they might not have, passengers can throw up, rideshare driving is not all "fun and games" and "great income."

I haven't had a passenger at risk for getting car sick since I stopped driving after midnight; however, my goal to not work after midnight was more about getting sleep... less drunks in my car was a nice side benefit.

o   Antacids (for me) too much fast food I guess?

o   Ibuprofen (for me) I don't want a little pain reducing my income, if my back is sore and I don't have a pain reliever I might think about quitting earlier than my plan.

o   Eyeglass and phone display cleaning spray (for me) When I drive in the morning or late afternoon the sun's reflection off a dirty phone screen can get in the way of seeing the navigation route. Working the TNC driver applications requires a lot off swiping across the screen, so my phone's display gets really dirty.

o   Breath spray (for me) I don't want to worry if I have bad breath.

o   Hand sanitizer (for me)

o   If you smoke tobacco, I would consider breath spray and hand sanitizer essential office tools.

Your non-smoking passengers will probably smell tobacco no matter what you do, many passengers are not going to be happy if your car reeks heavily of tobacco.

Strong tobacco smell might result in more four-star ratings, and if you receive frequent four-stars your average driver star rating score could approach the critical 4.6 rating and contact from the TNC support organization.

- **Things I think are nice to have:**

    o Bottled water (for passengers) I buy the cheapest I can find and have a couple of bottles in the front passenger door pocket, but I rarely offer them. Some passengers see the waters and ask if they can have one, occasionally a passenger will just help themselves as if there were a "free take one" sign, whatever, at $0.30 a bottle I never give it a second thought

    o Individually wrapped mints (for passengers) I like the soft peppermints, the ones that melt in your mouth, but it took a while before I stopped eating most of them myself. I've driven months with no mints in my car, and driven months always having a small zip-lock bag on the dash filled with soft mints. I rarely offer mints to passengers, if they ask great.

    o An additional phone charging cable including ability to charge iPhones and Android phones (for passengers, a relatively common request)

    ▪ I have an Android phone and have (rather "had") an adapter that converts Android to iPhone.

    Unfortunately, my adapter has been stolen by passengers twice. Recently I've driven months without the ability to charge an iPhone, and only have been asked for an iPhone charger a few times.

    Once, after saying "No" the passenger responded: "I once had a driver who had chargers for at least three types of phones."

    I was thinking: "Ok, and…?" Some passengers have expectations what every rideshare driver should have in their cars.

    I'm not concerned much about what other drivers do, this passenger's thinly-vailed attempt to make me feel guilty that I was not prepared to solve a problem he created did not affect my mood, it was only after he exited the car that I realized his statement: "*I once had a driver who had chargers for at least three types of phones...*" was probably intended to make me feel like I had failed and should go right out and buy a charging cable for every type of phone... "*Yeah, uh, no?*

Up to you as the driver, your office, your choice.

When people ask if I have a phone charger, it seems happened most often on a short trip, plugging into a car charger isn't going to help much during a five-minute ride? Maybe plan better, charge your phone?

iPhones do not have easily replaceable batteries and rechargeable batteries do not work as well when they are a few years old. If your iPhone-using passengers have older phones, are booking the cheapest-possible rideshare rides, is it really your responsibility to have a charger for their phones?

Also, interesting it's rare someone asks to charge an Android phone, given that over 80% smart phones worldwide run Android operating system... seems like there is something up with the iPhones needing charge?

- Note about passenger theft: Even if you know which passenger stole an item from your car, the passenger only has to deny stealing it when contacted by the TNC and you will not get it back or be reimbursed.

The moral is: Watch your stuff, or make sure you don't have valuable stuff in your car that is easy to steal. For example, my tip jar (a hat) is on my dash and mounted too high to make stealing from it easy. If someone stuck their hand in the tip hat, I would see it happen.

TAKING CARE OF YOUR RIDE

My rideshare vehicle is always "pretty darn clean" but I don't wash my car every day unless rain or snow has made the outside of the car really dirty and the current day's weather report says: "Fair skies ahead."

Inside my car the carpets are mostly clean/vacuumed, and the dash is not very dusty. I don't vacuum or wipe down the dashboard before every driving day.

I think I could dust the dash a bit more, but before rideshare driving I washed my car: "Once a year whether it needed it or not" and the front passenger seat looked like a messy closet. Every couple of years I would pay for a professional car wash and that's when the dash and inside of the windows would get cleaned.

Since I've been rideshare driving my car is never dirty on the outside unless rain/snow is in the forecast. And at least every couple of weeks I wipe the dust off the dash and clean the other interior surfaces with a wet rag.

It is far more important to take care of the mechanics of your rideshare vehicle, something I've always been good at doing. For example, the older Toyota Prius models have a tendency to consume oil, so I watch the oil level carefully.

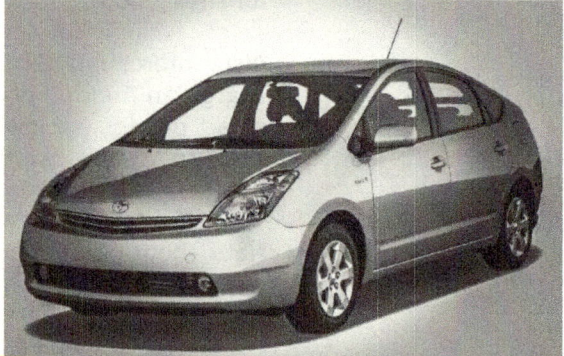

When I get oil changes I buy the more expensive synthetic blend oil. Since the more expensive oil is rated for about 9,000 miles (instead of 4,000) before the next oil change the overall cost is about the same.

I rideshare drive full-time, going longer between oil changes is an important benefit and I don't mind if I am paying a little extra because getting my oil changed means less time to earn.

I get my oil changed at my regular mechanic shop instead of a quick oil change shop in part because my mechanic's shop rotates the tires for no additional charge. Unlike the quick oil change shops I have to leave my car for a couple of hours, but I like the idea they are the only people taking care of my car's essential maintenance. My total time off the road is probably about the same because I don't have to visit one shop for an oil change and another shop for tire rotation.

I "tip" my mechanics with tasty adult beverages (cans not bottle, broken glass in a car shop is not cool.) I am a regular customer, I hope my "tips" mean the person doing the work is thinking well of me and taking good care of my car.

My Prius has a warning light for low tire pressure. If your vehicle doesn't have this feature (and even if it does) it is a good idea to check tire pressure regularly. Low tire pressure means lower average miles per gallon and less mileage on the tires before they need replacing.

If you don't have a trusted mechanic, I have used https://www.cars.com/dealers/service/ for decades to find highly rated repair shops close to where I live.

Final thoughts for this section, it has always been part of my car/truck buying plan to buy a quality used car or truck then put a lot of miles on it. I believe this is the most cost-effective choice for having a personal vehicle for my daily use.

Online reports typically put the annual cost of owning a family car at $8,000 to $9,000. Yes, that's every year.

This number makes sense to me only if calculating the real cost for starting with a brand-new car or truck. Five years after buying a new car or truck, the resale value will be about half of the brand-new price.

Using a $30,000 vehicle as example, the resale value goes down about 10% as soon as you drive it off the dealer's lot. That's about $3,000 depreciation for just driving the new car or truck home.

Research also says a new car or truck loses about 19% resale value in the first year of ownership. Calculating almost $6,000 lower resale value for a $30,000 new car or truck after the first year, and a total of about $15,000 lower resale value after five years, now an estimate of $8,000 to $9,000 annual cost of ownership doesn't sound completely unreasonable.

And we've only talked about reduction in resale value, add in fuel and maintenance costs and thinking about $8,000 to $9,000 annual cost of ownership starts to make sense.

Rideshare driving means putting greater than average miles on your vehicle. If a used vehicle has greater than 12,000 miles for every year it has been in service it will be considered a "high mileage vehicle," and the resale value will be lower.

The book: Driving for Uber and Lyft - How Much Can Drivers Earn? available from www.RideshareBusinessGuide.com provides all the math you need to calculate your exact rideshare driving take home pay including a detailed explanation how to calculate rideshare vehicle expense.

If you are considering using your vehicle to rideshare drive my best advice is to remember that your vehicle choice made sense to you at the time.

If you choose now to use the vehicle for rideshare driving, live with your car/truck choice for better and worse. In other words, if you are using a new vehicle to rideshare drive, live with the reality that your net earnings from rideshare driving will be less compared to starting with a vehicle you purchased used.

I purchased my last car with 95,000 miles and sold it with 215,000 miles on the odometer.

Then I purchased my rideshare driving vehicle, a 2006 Toyota Prius, with 98,000 miles on the odometer and it currently has over 250,000 miles. In my business plan I will drive the Prius to at least 300,000 miles and hopefully more.

Any way you slice it, owning a family car or truck is going to cost big bucks even if you are not using it for rideshare driving.

Rideshare driving means offsetting some of the expense of owning a vehicle by using it to generate income. Very helpful for offsetting overall income/expense the IRS gives rideshare drivers about $0.55 cents a mile tax deduction which drastically reduces the amount of rideshare driving income subject to taxation.

The book: Driving for Uber and Lyft - How Much Can Drivers Earn? available from www.RideshareBusinessGuide.com covers everything you need to know to calculate the expense of your rideshare driving vehicle including tax deductions and how much of your rideshare driving income to save to cover taxes, vehicle maintenance, and the depreciated value of your rideshare driving car, truck, or van.

THE BASICS OF RIDESHARE DRIVING EARNINGS

WHAT CAN YOU EARN AS A RIDESHARE DRIVER?

Judging by how often passengers ask, a lot of people are interested in knowing how much rideshare drivers earn. In my experience it is typical for people to want to equate rideshare driving earnings to an average hourly rate, the question I most often hear: "*How much do you earn per hour?*"

A Google search will return results to this question across the board.

The Transportation Network Companies or TNCs (think Uber and Lyft, etc.) give earnings per hour projections that are optimistic, and the wording of their hourly earning claims are... let's say carefully crafted.

In the past there have been successful false advertising lawsuits for misrepresenting what a rideshare driver can expect to earn and the TNCs have learned to be careful when talking about expected earnings.

The average earnings per hour I've seen reported from reputable research are typically significantly lower (by about $4 an hour) compared to the average hourly earnings I have seen while completing over 11,000 rideshare trips.

Trip Earnings Includes Surge, Boost, and tolls	$156.64
Tips	$12.00
Total Daily Earnings	**$168.64**

7hr 55min TIME ONLINE	18 TRIPS

| Earnings Help | |

TRIPS

1:09 AM UberX	$21.89 $16.89 + $5.00 Tip
12:56 AM UberX	$5.62
12:43 AM UberX	$7.12
12:29 AM UberX	$3.75 Canceled
12:12 AM UberX	$21.73
11:49 PM UberX	$8.54 $4.54 + $4.00 Tip
11:14 PM UberX	$3.75
10:54 PM UberX	$7.01
10:44 PM UberX	$3.75 Canceled
10:20 PM UberX	$3.75
10:05 PM UberX	$4.68
9:55 PM UberX	$6.75 $3.75 + $3.00 Tip
9:25 PM	$4.29

In rideshare driving forums and sites like Quora.com it is common to see rideshare drivers complaining that their average earnings after expenses are less than minimum wage. If that were true for me, I would have stopped rideshare driving and found a traditional job.

I suspect these reports of "less than minimum wage earnings" are not earnings averaged over weeks or even months; more likely worst-case scenarios.

It's also possible active rideshare drivers are giving their best guesses of their actual earnings because they are not going to the trouble of carefully tracking their earnings every day they drive.

I'd wager every rideshare driver on the road New Year's Eve or St. Patrick's Day will earn considerably more than minimum wage and personally I always earn significantly more than minimum wage; on a quiet Wednesday afternoon or a busy Friday night.

With many of the reports and articles sourced from current rideshare drivers I question if scientific research methods were used to compile results and draw conclusions? It's rare in these articles to see detailed explanations of the research methods used to compile the source data.

For example, a Toyota Prius gets better gas mileage and has a lower average maintenance cost compared to a Range Rover so it is not logical or accurate to lump together these drivers and suggest rideshare drivers in very different vehicles have comparable "take home pay."

Also missing in most articles is research criteria defining what kind of rideshare driver's experiences were surveyed.

For example, if the reported results were collected giving equal weight to:

1. The earnings of a soccer Mom/Dad rideshare driving a few hours a week during the day and trying to stay close to home... and
2. The earnings of a full-time rideshare driver working to maximize their income working during the busiest times for rideshare passenger trips transporting passengers anywhere in the city...

then the conclusions drawn and reported in the article will not reflect the reality of rideshare driving earnings.

In this example averages drawn from these very different categories of drivers will not accurately report expected income for either group... the reported average will be too high for the soccer mom/dad and too low for the driver out at night where there are more passenger trips.

Different types of rideshare drivers will have very different average hourly earnings; and the vehicle a given driver uses will also significantly affect "take home pay" after expenses.

Personally, I have meticulously tracked my daily/weekly/monthly average hourly earnings since my first day rideshare driving. What I've learned from analyzing this data helps me gauge how I am doing on a given day; but my primary focus is always on making enough money to pay my bills.

Focusing on how much income I'm taking home, my "take home pay", is far more important to me compared to focusing on my hourly average income on a given rideshare driving day.

The book Driving for Uber and Lyft - How Much Can Drivers Earn? references my Rideshare Earnings Case Study detailing my daily/weekly/monthly earnings reports for the 2017 & 2018 calendar years. This case study gives readers a good idea of what earnings per hour you may expect on a high earning day as well as a low earning day.

If you don't already have a copy of the case study send an email to wylee@ridesharebusinessguide.com and request a copy.

In summary, unfortunately no one can promise you what you will earn as a rideshare driver, an honest answer would be: "It depends."

- Being mentally prepared for the reality of income that varies from day to day will help when your earnings are less than what you hoped. Also true, when earnings are "great" realize that your earnings will average out over time.

- Figuring out exactly what you can earn working as a rideshare driver is complicated, complicated in part because the type of trips a driver gets is largely determined by luck.

- When a rideshare passenger requests a ride the TNC's software looks for the rideshare driver in the best position to arrive at the pick-up location first then offers the ride to that driver as a Trip Request. The passenger might be going just around the corner or they might be going across town.

- If the rideshare driver accepts the passenger's Trip Request the TNC's smart phone application gives navigation directions to the pick-up location without providing the passenger's destination in advance.

DRIVERS DON'T KNOW WHERE A PASSENGER IS GOING BEFORE THEY PICK THEM UP?

Yes, this is true, and while this reality may not seem ideal for drivers it makes a lot of sense for rideshare passengers.

As a seasoned rideshare driver if I knew a potential passenger was going on a very short trip it is unlikely I would drive over 10 minutes to get to the pick-up location knowing I will make less than four dollars gross income for my total time spent completing the trip.

Rideshare passengers going on short trips might have a difficult time getting picked up at all.

The TNC's have said they don't show drivers the destination address before the rideshare driver has arrived at the pick-up location in part because of "Destination Prejudice."

When I first heard this, I immediately thought about cities where there are neighborhoods with the reputation of being unsafe and thought it makes sense some rideshare drivers would not want passenger drop-off locations in parts of town they avoid in their personal driving.

Thankfully, in Denver where I drive there are few places with that kind of reputation.

Consider this: I wrote previously I would not drive a long distance to a pick-up location for a short ride... ironically that is exactly destination prejudice, just not for the reason that first came to my mind. I would be screening out trips where my current location and the passenger's final destination meant I wouldn't earn a lot of income for my time.

So unfortunately, the rideshare driver does not know where the next trip will take them before the passenger pick-up but passengers benefit by getting drivers to accept their shorter trips.

I would argue that rideshare drivers benefit too because if rideshare passengers had a difficult time getting a rideshare driver for a short trip it is unlikely they would count on rideshare transportation for longer trips, trips which are significantly more profitable for rideshare drivers.

Final thought here, remember hourly earnings average out over time; rideshare drivers complete short, medium, and long trips, it is all part of the rideshare driving gig.

WHAT CAN YOU EARN AS A RIDESHARE DRIVER? – Part Two

When a driver completes a short trip, (the TNCs call this a "Minimum Fare" trip), the driver earns less than $4.00 before expenses. In contrast when completing a longer trip the fare is calculated based on distance and time so the rideshare driver completing a longer trip will earn considerably more gross income during a given time-period compared to completing a few short trips.

This brief discussion of rideshare driving income is meant to set context for later contents of this book... the primary focus in this volume is the practical, day-to-day aspects of being a rideshare driver... to understand all of the financial aspects of your rideshare driving business I recommend getting a copy of <u>Driving for Uber and Lyft - How Much Can Drivers Earn?</u> available from <u>RideshareBusinessGuide.com</u>.

MAKE MORE MONEY - SURGE PRICING, BONUS OFFERS, AND PROMOTIONS

"Travelers, there is no path, paths are made by walking." Antonio Machado

There are a number of ways rideshare drivers see additional earnings added to trips and paychecks including Surge Pricing; Earnings Promotions; and occasionally a Bonus you can earn by satisfying the requirements of the Bonus offer.

SURGE ZONE PRICING

Surge Zones happen when the TNC's software is expecting more Trip Requests than there are online drivers in Surge Pricing area. The TNC online trainings tell drivers to drive into Surge Zones for the opportunity to get Trip Requests with Surge Pricing.

Surge Zone pricing, also called "dynamic fare pricing" is not an exact science and it is possible to think you are in a Surge Zone then get a Trip Request for normal fare pricing. Unless you see surge pricing displayed on the Trip Request or in the TNC driver application you will not know if a given trip has Surge Pricing added until after the trip is completed.

Once I had a passenger who insisted Surge Pricing zones were being controlled by live TNC resources sitting in a room somewhere.

There is simply no way this could be true; Surge Pricing zones are controlled by software logic.

I didn't bother to walk this passenger through the error in his logic by asking him to explain how it would be possible or why Uber, Lyft, and the other transportation network companies would be willing to pay live human beings to do something that could easily be programmed into computers.

When I was a new rideshare driver, I followed the advice offered in the TNC online trainings and when I saw a Surge Pricing Zone displayed on the TNC driver application map I would navigate toward the zone.

Almost every time I chased a Surge Pricing zone I either saw the Surge Pricing zone disappear from the map before or immediately after my car's icon entered the displayed zone.

Sometimes I would get a Trip Request thinking I would get paid greater than standard rates but after completing the trip seeing in my trip history I only made my standard pay for mileage and time.

Sometimes I would enter the area displayed on the application map but I did not get an immediate Trip Request.

This confused me, if there were more passengers wanting rides and not enough drivers to accept their Trip Requests then why wasn't I getting a Trip Request?

In many cases I sat waiting for 5, 10, 15 minutes but did not get any trips requests until the Surge Pricing zone disappeared completely from the TNC application map.

As a new driver trying to figure out the best way to get my next Trip Request and maximize my income my experience with Surge Pricing zones was very frustrating.

After chasing Surge Pricing and waiting without a Trip Request... finally I would get a normal fare Trip Request and found myself thinking I had: [1] wasted time traveling to the Surge Pricing Zone; [2] wasted time waiting for a Trip Request; [3] then when I finally got a trip I was paid my standard time and distance rates.

Again, very frustrating for a new driver.

When I drive now, I pretty much ignore Surge Pricing Zones unless there is a good reason to believe the Surge Pricing will persist.

For example, when a sporting event or concert is ending the Surge Pricing Zone is likely not going away quickly because passengers know they can't just wait the Surge Pricing out and request a trip once there are more drivers in the area and the Surge Pricing goes down or disappears completely.

When Surge Pricing shows on the TNC customer application savvy passengers will sometimes walk a few blocks trying to get out of the Surge Pricing zone.

From a driver's perspective, if I drop off a passenger and see there is active Surge Pricing in the zone where I'm currently located, I usually will pull over somewhere and wait for at least 5 minutes to see if I get a Trip Request.

Another thing I do might not make sense at first... if the Surge Pricing is really high, like 3.5x over normal fares, I might drive away from the Surge Pricing zone.

Three and a half times no Trip Requests equals... you got it, no income.

As I said previously, Surge Pricing may behave differently in the city where you drive. Passengers have told me in large cities like Chicago, New York, San Francisco, etc. there are parts of town that on a busy Friday or Saturday night will have Surge Pricing all night long.

As example a passenger from Washington DC told me: *"In DC, if we see Surge Pricing of only 1.8x normal fare we will grab it quick before it goes higher."*

If you choose to be a rideshare driver you will make your own choices.

Armed will a bit more information than a driver trying to figure out rideshare driving by themselves, hopefully you won't get frustrated like I did when I would drive 10 minutes or more to get to a Surge Pricing zone only to see the zone disappear before or right after I entered it.

Since there is no way to know what passengers requesting trips or the other TNC drivers are doing in a given moment there is no way to know what will happen when you find yourself in a Surge Pricing zone.

PROMOTIONS

Promotions are typically guaranteed higher fares in a specific part of town during a specific time period.

As example on a Friday or Saturday night; in downtown Denver; near clusters of bars and restaurants; and after midnight it is a pretty good bet for the TNCs there will be greater than average Trip Requests so a promotion for drivers makes sense.

And there are drivers like me would rather be home by midnight so might not stay out on the road for late night rideshare driving unless there is a good reason like a guaranteed way to earn higher than standard fare rates.

Also true, if my last trip's drop-off location was away from the known hot spots, out in the suburbs, I'm not going to rush back into town unless there is a really good reason to do so.

If there are Promotions in play they might give me a good reason to head immediately back to a particular part of town.

It usually takes a good promotion to keep me on the road late at night... 1.2x over standard fares (20% increase) is unlikely to motivate me to work the early morning hours unless it was already a part of my plan for the week.

Guaranteed 1.4x standard fares might motivate me but it usually takes a better offer to make me change my plans or drive empty from the suburbs to the downtown area chasing a TNC Promotion.

Bear in mind that just because there is an active Promotion does not mean you will get many Trip Requests or possibly any Trip Requests at all.

On a recent Friday night Uber was offering guaranteed 2.1x normal fare (so more than double standard fares) from midnight to 2 a.m. for trips where the pick-up location was in the downtown Denver area as defined by a circle displayed on the TNC driver application map.

2.1x normal fare means a Minimum Fare trip will be almost $8 compared to less than $4. Even if I'm getting only Minimum Fare trips $8 a trip is interesting money and if I score a longer trip 2.1x normal fare turns a $20 trip into an over $40 trip.

At about 11:30 p.m. I was feeling tired and had already been on the road for eight hours, I stayed online but started working my way toward home.

On my way home, I accepted a Trip Request with a drop-off location in downtown Denver right in the middle of the 2.1x over normal fares Promotion zone.

Now it was almost midnight, so I decided to stick around hoping to get at least one 2.1x fare before going offline and heading home. I was hoping to "score" at least a medium-length trip adding $20 or more to my earnings for the day.

I parked my car in front of Denver's Union Station (the heart of Denver's LoDo hotspot) and waited.

At this location my car was in the middle of the Promotion zone and I waited there listening to the radio for about 20 minutes with no Trip Requests.

Thinking I might have better luck if my car was moving, I circled around passing the hottest of the hot spots in LoDo and nearby RiNo neighborhoods.

Finally, almost a full hour later, I got a Trip Request with pick-up location less than a block away from my current location.

I pulled up to the curb, a woman came up to my window telling me her friend had too much to drink and asked me if I minded getting him home. From the way she phrased her question I assumed she meant "pouring" her intoxicated friend into my car by himself and the really drunk guy would be the only passenger.

I was thankful she asked; in my experience in a situation like this one, it is more common to feel like I'm having the falling-down-drunk person forced on me.

More often the more-sober person phrases their request sounding like an order: *"You are going to take my really drunk friend home."*

If someone sounds like they are telling me I have to do something, I have no choice, it is very easy for me to say: *"No."*

I was thankful to have my personal rideshare driving business unbreakable rules (more on this later, for now know I will never take a falling down drunk passenger home unless someone rides along to "babysit") and I replied: *"No thank you."* I rolled up my windows, drove away, then canceled the Trip Request. Since the passenger was there at my window before the trip was eligible for a cancellation fee I earned nothing.

Now it was past 1 a.m. and I've earned nothing for an hour and a half of my time. I was feeling tried but now I wanted to make something to justify my decision to stay out and earn "*a little more.*"

I got another Trip Request and the pick-up location was only a couple of blocks away from my current location. The pick-up location was in front of a popular bar and judging by the people coming and going and standing outside the bar it was very busy Inside.

I waited 4 minutes for the passenger to arrive, passengers have 5 minutes before they can be charged a cancellation fee.

After 4 minutes it is my custom to call passengers on the phone: "*Hello this is your driver I'm at your location.*" The man who answered the phone sounded a little drunk and it was very loud in the background, he asked me where I was but didn't specifically say what he planned to do; it sounded like he was coming out to the car, so I continued to wait.

Side note: When I don't have to drive very far to the pick-up location I am usually more willing to let a passenger keep me waiting after the trip is eligible for a cancellation fee. Plus, in this case, I knew I would be making 2.1x normal fare for the trip so could be worth the longer wait.

After waiting another 3 minutes I called the passenger again and said: "*Hello this is your driver do you still need a ride*?" He responded, "*Where are you again*?"; Me: "*In front of the Viewhouse bar*" he said simply: "*No*" and hung up. I cancelled the Trip Request choosing "Cancel/No Show" and made $3.75.

So now instead of being home on my easy chair over an hour ago I'd spent midnight to after 1 a.m. earning just $3.75. I was feeling like I made the wrong decision.

I decided to head for home but stayed online still hoping to get a 2.1x fare. I was approaching the entrance to the highway home and got a Trip Request about 5 minutes away and for 2.1x over normal fare - yippee!

When I picked the passengers up they were not noticeably drunk (bonus) however the passengers were going to the Southeast side of Denver and my house is Northwest of town, so the trip to the drop-off location took me pretty far away from my home.

There is always risk when you are ready to go home (and not using the TNC application Destination feature) the Trip Request you accept will be taking you farther from home. In this case the trip took me quite a bit farther from home.

A good rule of thumb I usually follow: If I'm tired and ready to call it quits for the day I go offline and drive home.

I still put this experience in the win zone because I earned $40 for the single trip so $43.75 for about two hours of my time and the alternative was earning only $3.75 for the one cancelled trip in almost the same amount of time.

True I stayed out about two hours after I wanted to be home for the night but if I earn at least $18 an hour for my time, I'm always happy. In this case I earned over $20 an hour.

For months now instead of working after midnight I start early, about 2 p.m. By starting early, I can skip driving during the wee hours of the morning.

I started doing this because it felt like I was tired a lot of the time from staying up late, but it is also true that before midnight passengers seem to be a bit more predictable and after midnight, well... my Mom used to tell me: "*Nothing good happens after midnight*!"

Well I can't agree with "nothing good" but in my experience working after midnight as a rideshare driver there is a greater chance of "interesting" things happening.

When I was a new driver, I remember feeling really frustrated working the midnight to 2 a.m. hours and sometimes only getting a few Minimum Fare trips. Working late and making only a little extra money did not feel good at all.

BONUS OFFERS

The TNC Bonus offer requirements are usually straight-forward and often a relatively easy way to increase earnings.

The TNCs are constantly experimenting with different Bonus offers and it is not uncommon to see a particular type of Bonus used a couple of times and then never again.

The Bonus offers I like best are "X" dollars added to my TNC paycheck for completing "X" rides over a full calendar week or sometimes the time frame is over a weekend. These Bonus offers, sometimes called Quest Bonuses are usually easy to understand and relatively easy to meet the requirements.

If the Bonus offer is "X" completed trips during a shorter time frame, say 4 hours, I use 2 trips per hour to calculate if I think the Bonus offer is achievable during the hours I plan to drive.

I know I might be able to average 3 or even 4 trips per hour but one long trip could put the Bonus earnings out of reach. When I'm considering trying to earn the Bonus I think: "2 trips per hour."

In my experience a TNC Bonus offer in a short time period will not motivate me to change my driving plan or my normal habits. I will still have the Bonus in mind as possible to earn, but I am also thinking:

"If I earn the Bonus great if not then oh well."

Important note: I almost always use my calculator to determine if a Bonus offer will pay a compelling amount of money before I make a plan to pursue it.

For example, if a Bonus offer is $22 for 31 completed rides then the Bonus is only adding about $0.70 for each completed ride, not a very compelling amount of money.

Some Bonus offers will add two or more dollars for every completed ride, I am more likely to pursue an offer where I will earn an additional $2 for every ride.

I typically think about Minimum Fare trips, normally about $3.40 an extra two dollars per trip puts each Minimum Fare trip over $5. If I have a good chance of making at least $5 for each short ride I've got a pretty good chance of meeting or exceeding my $20+ dollar an hour average earnings.

With the "X" rides during "X" time frame... if I don't earn the Bonus it probably means I completed more longer trips and probably made as much if not more than if I'd earned the Bonus.

Remember the types of Trip Requests you get will always contain a particle of luck.

The TNC's are always creating new ways to motivate rideshare drivers to drive when and where it makes sense for the TNC.

Approaching the rideshare driving gig with a professional mindset you will have to decide whether or not to change your driving plan and habits.

Always remember, earnings average out over time so don't let a Bonus offer or Promotion be your only guide for where and when to drive.

Since I started going home around midnight I am choosing not to pursue the late night/wee hours Bonus offers almost every Friday and Saturday night I drive.

Sometimes I think: "*I could stay out and earn more?*" But I remind myself that I might stay out and only earn a little extra money or maybe nothing, so I usually resist the urge and go home.

After almost three years of driving I've learned how to take care of myself and make my own choices about when and where I drive.

It took a while for me to think more about putting in enough hours to make my earning goals and not "chase" options I think might yield greater than average hourly earnings.

I always average around $20 an hour, if I drive 40 hours I will earn about $800 gross income.

ADDITIONAL THOUGHTS ABOUT SURGES, PROMOTIONS, and BONUSES

The TNC's offer additional money for the same work because they are trying to get drivers to do something they are concerned drivers would not do without the possibility of additional earnings.

For example, Boulder, Colorado has around 30,000 college students who are mostly out of town for about a month over Winter Break. Boulder is about 45 minutes from downtown Denver and a contained community meaning rideshare passengers in Boulder are typically only requesting a trip to another part of Boulder; so mostly short trips and likely lower average hourly earnings.

- When the college students are out of town there are significantly less Trip Requests so the TNCs will offer

Promotions to insure there will be enough drivers to meet passenger requests.

- Since the TNC's don't have direct control over driver behavior there could be too many drivers for available trips because of the Promotion offer.
- I've been "burned" more than once driving in a Promotion Zone but getting little to no Trip Requests – 2.1x fares times zero trips equals zero earnings.
- Typically, new drivers (not armed with the information in this book) haven't figured out yet that the TNCs might be offering the Promotion because without it the wait times for a Trip Request are likely to be very long for passengers.

In the city where you drive you may know or discover parts of town where most passengers are likely to mostly request trips only going a short distance. Discovering these places can be helpful if you want to knock out a few short trips before going home or are working toward a Bonus based on getting a certain number of trips in a certain time frame.

On the other hand, if you are hoping for longer trips so higher average hourly earnings, you might choose to avoid these areas.

I won't chase a Surge Price Zone, meaning drive a significant distance to reach the Surge Pricing Zone, but if I find myself in one I typically will hang out for at least a while.

Finding yourself in a Surge Zone might be a really good time to take a break while staying online ready to accept a Trip Request, get out of your car and stretch your legs.

Repeating from earlier, if the Surge Pricing is really high, like 3.5x normal fare, I might choose to drive away from the Surge Pricing zone.

- Imagine you are a passenger about to request a trip and the TNC passenger application tells you the trip, you normally take for a $10 fare, is going to cost you $35? You probably would choose to see if you could wait out the Surge Pricing too?

- Newer drivers will be flocking to the Surge Pricing zone and the Surge Pricing will go down or even disappear completely as soon as there are enough drivers in the area to satisfy the TNC's anticipated increase in Trip Requests.

Remember that Surge Pricing zones vary from city to city. In Denver it is unusual for Surge Pricing to persist more than 15-20 minutes and I've seen times after a big event, even with tons of people requesting rides… no Surge Pricing in play.

Remember the TNC psychology resources I mentioned earlier, it always makes sense to question why a particular TNC Promotion or Bonus offer might be in play... you may want to do something other than what the promotion offer is attempting to motivate you to do.

If you see Surge Pricing zones on the TNC driver's application map you might point your car in that direction, but it probably makes sense to stay online and be happy when you get a Trip Request, Surge Pricing or no.

Earn the extra income if you can but make your own choices when and where to drive.

In my twenties, for about seven years, I worked at about a dozen different bars and restaurants as a waiter and a bartender. I was always hearing stories that waiters/bartenders at some other restaurant or bar were making money "hand over fist."

More than once I made the switch to another restaurant, to what I hoped would be "greener grass" only to find that the money I earned at the new place was more or less the same as the place I just left.

The point I want to make: As a rideshare driver it is all too easy to think: "*I should have done [whatever] and I probably would have made more money.*"

The lesson I've learned is to try to not second guess myself, I did what I did and I made what I made, when I average out my hourly earnings over time I am always happy with my average rideshare driving income.

Remember that TNC Surges, Promotions, and Bonuses are offered to get drivers to do things they might not normally do so these extra earnings are not offered without "Strings attached."

- Make sure you read the offer details closely to avoid, for example, thinking you are driving in a Promotion Zone that is only being offered only to food delivery drivers or you think the offer is active, but it ended hours ago.

- It makes sense to have proof of the offer (a screenshot works) in case you think you should have been paid extra but were not. It is very common for TNC support resources to ask you to upload a copy of the Promotion or Bonus offering.

- There is no way to prove or disprove Surge Pricing because the offers are dynamic. Typically, I will not argue with TNC support resources over Surge Pricing, if I get extra earnings great and if not: "Oh well."

Every week I get at least a few trips that include additional earnings however I don't count on Surges, Promotions, or Bonuses to make my rideshare driving living; I know that the additional money will improve my average earnings for the week but when I'm planning my week I'm always thinking: *"If I drive at least 40 hours then I will make at least $800"*, more times than not I earn more.

WHERE WILL I FIND MY NEXT TRIP?

"The only real voyage of discovery consists not in seeking new landscapes but in having new eyes." Marcel Proust

I wish I could tell you a sure-fire way to always find your next Trip Request soon after you drop off your last passengers. If I had a secret way to find trips I would share it, rideshare drivers aren't really competing with each other for passenger trips. If I had discovered a sure-fire way to "land the next one," I could use the method to find my next trip too.

The good news, it's rare that I have to "look" for my next Trip Request; the next passenger trip usually finds me soon after I drop my last passenger off. During high-traffic times of day/night I often get the next request before the current trip is done.

When I first started rideshare driving I thought I had to "search" for my next trip and I would try to think like a taxi driver: "Where should I go to catch my next trip?"

If the last passenger's drop-off location was deep in the suburbs I'd wonder: *"Should drive back into the city?"* or *"Should I pull over and wait?"* or *"Should I hang out near the closest hotel?"*

An important distinction to understand, in most cities, laws designed to protect the highly-regulated taxi industry, forbid drivers for Uber, Lyft, Taxify, and the other TNCs to solicit passenger rides or be "flagged down" by a passenger.

All rideshare Trip Requests must come from the TNC rideshare driver applications.

If someone tries to flag you down and offers to pay cash for a ride you are taking a big risk if you agree. You are probably breaking at least one city law and you are taking chances with your personal safety.

Taxi drivers don't have any information about their passengers, don't know even the passenger's first name and unless the passenger pays with a credit card, all they have at the end of a ride is "a fare."

Rideshare drivers have an advantage over taxis because, in order to request a ride, rideshare passengers must have a valid credit card on file with the TNC. The fact that someone is "on the hook" as a known, trackable person helps protect rideshare driver's safety.

Also true, if you choose to transport someone for cash, working outside of the TNC application, you are not covered by the TNC's insurance policy and probably not covered by your personal insurance policy either.

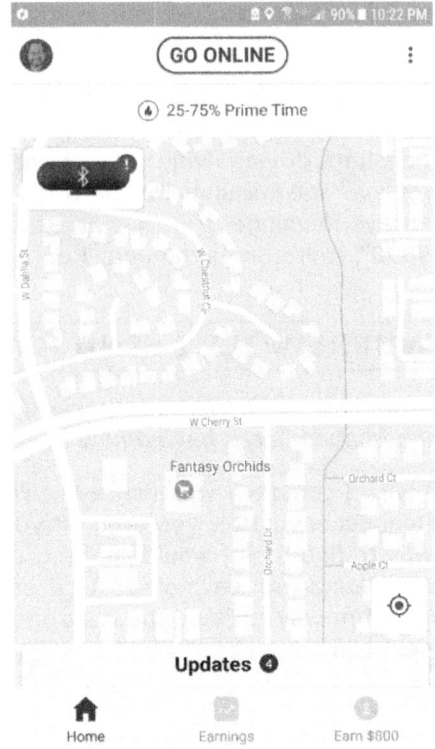

Personal insurance policies that include rideshare coverage are priced based on the reality that the TNC insurance policies cover rideshare drivers in two of the three stages of rideshare driving:

1. Covered – from the moment you accept a Trip Request

2. Covered – while a passenger is in your car and engaged in an active TNC trip, before the driver chooses the "End Trip" option

3. Not covered – As soon as you select the "End Trip" option until you accept your next trip, it's best not to formally end a trip until all passengers have exited your car and closed the doors

If your personal insurance company learns you were transporting a stranger for cash, they may refuse to pay a claim. They would be well within their rights because personal insurance includes covering you as a rideshare driver will spell these realities out.

If your personal insurance had liability when you are driving to a pick-up location and/or transporting a passenger in your car, the price of the policy would be higher – a lot higher.

Taxi drivers must collect cash or credit card payment at the end of a trip, rideshare transportation is a "transaction free" experience, the financial transactions happen through the rideshare application and drivers are not directly involved.

Rarely a passenger will ask me a question about their fare, I can truthfully answer: *"Drivers are not involved in the financial transaction, you will have to contact the TNC [Uber, Lyft, Taxify, etc.]"*

YOUR NEXT TRIP REQUEST

Back to the topic of finding your next trip.

When I first started rideshare driving, I would drop off a passenger and try to think like a taxi driver then navigate toward a place I thought I might get my next Trip Request. I was just guessing, I didn't have any good information to guide my actions.

Often it seemed I would receive Trip Requests with pick-up locations in almost the same place as my last drop-off location. In other words, I might drive 10 minutes toward a place I hoped I'd get my next Trip Request, then find myself driving 8 minutes back in the direction I had just left.

Some rideshare driving blogs, websites, and YouTube channels try to provide "Hot Tips" how to find your next Trip Request, I've not found their tips to be much help.

The reality is your next Trip Request is more about luck and timing than anything else. When someone requests a trip through the TNC application, and you are the closest driver, the Trip Request is presented to you through the TNC driver application.

When I "settled down" and stopped trying to chase my next Trip Request, stopped trying to think like a taxi driver, my stress level went down, and interestingly my average hourly earnings went up.

Another important thought: remember the reality of statistics, it takes more than a couple of coin tosses to end up with an even number of heads or tails results and it takes more than a few hours of doing anything as a rideshare driver before a clear trend will emerge.

In the case of rideshare driving, this means that a couple of hours or even a couple of days of "experiences" are probably not statistically significant.

As example, when I started driving rideshare, I thought driving in the suburbs was not the most profitable and I made this decision based on only a few days of driving in the suburbs.

A few hours of driving doesn't "prove" anything! I've made great hourly averages without leaving the suburbs, the pick-up locations tend to be a little farther away but in return the length of the trips tends to be longer.

In the next few pages I share my suggestions for finding Trip Requests. For now, I suggest relaxing about finding next trips and think about the law of averages – rideshare earnings will average out over time.

Rideshare drivers complete short, medium, and longer trips, the length of the trips you get are largely based on luck.

You will have "great" earning days, and you will have days that are not as good, over time you will figure out an average hourly rate where you drive.

My average hourly rate for at least the past year-and-a-half, is around $20 gross income per hour, usually more.

LIVING WITH VARIABLE TRIP EARNINGS - THE FISHING ANALOGY

After months of rideshare driving it occurred to me that finding my next Trip Request could be compared to fishing. This analogy helped reduce my stress about my future rideshare driver earnings.

When I was a boy, my grandfather would take me fishing in the streams, ponds, and lakes of East Texas. We stored the fish we caught in a large green mesh basket with a spring-loaded lid on the top.

When I think about finding my next trip I imagine I'm fishing with a net instead of a bamboo pole, string, hook, and worm. A rideshare driver's "net" is essentially from their current location to anywhere they can drive in average 10 minutes or less, usually less than 10 minutes from current location.

If my grandfather and I were fishing in streams, most of the catch was Perch (also called Bluegill or Brim.) Perch are not large fish (excepting the Nile Perch) but at the end of the day we usually had a nice pile of fish in our basket.

If we fished in a pond or lake, we might also catch larger fish like Carp, Catfish, and hopefully a few Smallmouth or Largemouth Bass. As a boy I would dream of catching lots of nice-sized Bass, maybe even a trophy Bass, one that weighed a few pounds; however, most of the time, at the end of the day, our big green basket would contain mostly Perch, less than a pound each, with a few larger fish in the mix.

When I'm rideshare driving I think of the variety of trips (short, medium, and longer) as being similar to my childhood fishing experiences.

Most days I will have a bunch of Minimum Fare trips along with a few trips a few dollars over a Minimum Fare trip (think Perch/Bluegill/Brim.) Mix in a few medium-length trips; and hopefully a longer trip or two (Carp/Catfish/Bass.)

Like my boyhood fishing experiences, at the end of most days, my "basket" is "filled" with an interesting amount of money or to complete the analogy, "fish."

At the end of most of my rideshare driving day I'm going home with a non-trivial amount of money.

Remember I'm always focused on how much income I'm producing and not my average hourly rate. Certainly, I look at my average hourly rate, and track it in a spreadsheet but my daily, weekly, monthly income goals are always measured in amount of earnings needed to pay my bills.

90

On a given night, my average hourly earnings indicates how well I've done that rideshare driving shift, so also of interest. The math is simple, the end of each shift I divide my total earnings by my total time online to calculate my average hourly rate for the shift.

> A quick note about tracking your hours: When I take time to eat, or when I take a "real" break, I take the TNC application(s) offline and I "punch out." Expecting to be "paid" for the total hours you are away from home, in my opinion, is not accurately tracking your earnings as a rideshare driver.

> Of course, how you track your hours is your choice; however, an accurate account of your average hourly income can be very helpful for planning approximately how many hours your need to work to make your goal amount of income.

There are free smart phone applications designed to track contractor work hours; I suggest finding one you like and using it every time you drive.

I use an Android application called "Worklog Pro" and upgraded from the free to the paid version to have access to downloadable reports. I punch in right before I go online, punch out when I'm done driving, and Worklog Pro has a place to record my breaks.

At the end of a shift, I usually don't count all of my travel time home.

As example if I am offline and drive 30 minutes home I typically only count about 15 minutes of my "commute" time going home from working. My thinking is a traditional job is going to include some unpaid commuting time so a "fairer" accounting of my average hourly rate rideshare driving should not include all of the time it takes me to get home.

So again when I'm "fishing" for rides, I imagine I am using a "net" that covers a pretty large area.

I imagine the size of my rideshare driving "net" to be about 10-12 minute drive in any direction from my current location.

In other words, if I'm sitting in a parking lot waiting for the next Trip Request most Trip Requests will be no more than a 10 to 12 minute drive from my current location, it's more common for them to be about 5 minutes away from my current location.

RIDESHARE AVERAGE HOURLY EARNINGS

During the over two years I've been rideshare driving, completing over 11,000 trips, my average hourly earnings have tracked consistently at $16-$18 an hour during weekdays daytime hours; and $20-$22 average per hour driving afternoons, after 4 p.m. into the night.

I drive a mix of daytime and nighttime hours, and for my income planning I use $20 an hour. If I drive 40 hours in a week I know I will earn approximately $800, sometimes a little more and sometimes a little less.

Of course, I've had rideshare driving shifts with much higher average hourly earnings as well as shifts where I've experienced lower earnings; over time my average hourly income results have been consistently in the $20 an hour range. At the end of a shift I'm happy with anything over average $18 an hour.

It's only because I have taken the time to accurately tracked my hours online, as well as my total income per shift, that I know rideshare driving earnings average out over time. I've looked at the data over weeks and months, my average earnings are always consistent.

When I have a stellar earning shift, I don't get overly excited anymore. I'm happy to have had a high-earning shift but I know that I will have some lower earning shifts too.

I use my average hourly earnings over time to guide how many hours I am going to drive; if I put in the hours online, I know I will earn the money I need to pay my bills.

Here are some other thoughts and suggestions regarding getting your next trip:

- When I'm driving at night it's very common to accept my next Trip Request before dropping off my current passengers. Starting at about 4 p.m. going through the night I am consistently busy accepting and completing trips.
  - When I have passengers in my car I typically accept 100% of Trip Requests I am offered, I can always "Cancel/No Charge" after the current passenger's drop-off. I don't want to take my eyes and mental focus off the road.

- When I am waiting for my next Trip Request I sometimes park in a location with easy access to quickly move in multiple directions.

- If I'm not parked, I am almost always navigating toward somewhere using the GPS application, or at least driving with a general destination in mind, when I am driving and waiting for my next Trip Request, the direction I drive is rarely random.

- If the last passenger drop-off location was deep in a neighborhood, away from a major intersection. I will almost always use the GPS application as if I were navigating home or toward Downtown Denver. Using the GPS application gives me navigation directions which will get me out of the neighborhood and to a major road, using the GPS application prevents me from circling around trying to find my way out from memory.
    - o   I often get my next Trip Request before getting to the main road or soon after.

- The practice of social engineering can be useful finding the next Trip Request, I think:
"What are a lot of people likely to be doing right now? Where might a lot of people be coming from or going to right now?"
    - o   In the early evening hours, people are more likely to be going out to restaurants or bars, so I won't hang out by the hot spot zones; instead I drive away from the hot spots into places where people are more likely to be coming from, so residential areas.
    - o   After about 9 p.m. I will drive toward the hot spots thinking people are more likely to be going home or at least going to a different hot spot.

- If I'm moving and still waiting for my next Trip Request I typically avoid highways.
    - o   I have gotten lots of Trip Requests while driving on the highway but if I'm waiting for my next Trip Request I usually believe I have a better chance when moving slower. Give the "fish" time to swim into your "net."

- I am almost always navigating toward somewhere; downtown Denver might be a 30-minute drive but I'm heading in that direction.
    - o   I don't expect to drive 30 minutes before receiving the next Trip Request, but if I don't get a Trip Request I will end up in a location likely to produce trips.

- I usually stay online when I'm traveling toward a location, I'm just hoping a moving vehicle might have a better chance of catching the next Trip Request.

o This doesn't mean I'm less likely to get a Trip Request sitting in a parking lot, sometimes I don't feel like sitting and waiting, so I drive.

- If there are Promotions or Bonus offers I am working to earn, or if there are Surge Pricing Zones I believe will persist, I might go offline and take the shortest route back to a location where I hope I will improve my chance of earning the extra income.
    - o There have been times where I have felt this strategy has not paid off. If I don't have my next Trip Request, I am always making my best guess what to do, where to go, or not go. I try not to second guess myself and remember that earnings average out over time.

Of course, it would be nice if there were a perfect way to find the next Trip Request, a method rideshare drivers could figure out then repeat over and over. The reality is when a passenger requests a trip the TNC application simply looks for the closest available driver and sends the Trip Request to that driver's phone.

HOT TIP: Save TNC phone numbers in your phone's contact/address book to identify the numbers for Caller ID. The TNCs use a rotating block of phone numbers, I currently have 30+ Uber phone numbers saved. The numbers are named "UBER 01"; "UBER 02", etc. and when I get a phone call in advance of arriving at the next Passenger's Pick-Up Location the Caller ID let's me know it is an Uber Passenger calling.

WHEN TO DRIVE

What times of day you choose to drive will almost always affect your average earnings for the given timeframe. Typically, afternoons after 4 p.m. into the night will produce more Trip Requests compared to say 11 a.m. to 3 p.m.

That said, one longer trip can make a daytime shift's average hourly earnings as good or even better than the busier afternoon/evening shifts. Remember luck will always be a contributing factor.

The TNCs will communicate when are the best times to drive, by email and notifications through the driver applications. When a TNC communicates "a good time to drive" they mean time periods where there are likely to be greater than average passenger Trip Requests.

Uber and Lyft agree on two good times to drive Monday-Friday: from 6 a.m. to 9 a.m. and from 4 p.m. to 7 p.m. basically common commuter times – rush hours.

Obviously, Friday and Saturday nights are usually busy, and in general anytime more people are out having fun.

Not as obvious but also a good time to drive: 3:30 a.m. to sunup because of trips to the airport. Of course, if you are located close to the airport these rides will be just another trip.

Assuming the airport in your city is a good distance from the location you start driving (most drivers start "work" near their home) then airport rides will mean a good fare.

In Denver a trip to the airport is almost always at least $20 income for the driver and from Boulder County or the densely populated southern suburbs a single trip can mean a $30+ fare.

Remember, think about what most people are doing right now (social engineering), as example, airport passengers catching redeye flights are overrepresented in the "wee hours" and there are typically less rideshare drivers on the road.

Think about business travelers, they usually leave early in the week and travel home late in the week. Rides from residential areas to the airport are more likely early Monday and Tuesday mornings, and rides from hotels to the airport are more likely early Thursday and Friday mornings.

Few flights are landing around 6 a.m. so you if you drop a passenger at the airport early you probably will have to drive away from the airport with an empty car. However, during a busier time of day for incoming flights, getting a Trip Request out of the airport after dropping a passenger off can mean good earnings in a relatively short period of time.

If you choose to work the early morning hours you can catch the morning commute time too.

Big events like professional sports; concerts; conventions; etc. increase rideshare travel but I'm not a fan of picking up after a sporting event or concert. Slow-moving traffic and pedestrians blocking traffic are the norm after a big event and it can be hard to find your passengers in the large crowds of people waiting for a rideshare pick-up.

When I first started driving I would avoid the end of large events. In my driving now, I don't really avoid the end of large events, but I'm not purposefully trying to be close either. Yes, there is often Surge Pricing after a big event, but more than once I've gotten short rides with a drop-off location at a relatively close bar or restaurant, after spending greater than average time finding a passenger.

I've also gotten more than a few trips after the end of a big event to a relatively close drop-off location - where the passenger parked their car. These passengers find somewhere cheap or free to park close to the event location and use rideshare transportation to get to and from the event.

Don't be surprised when passengers saving money on parking don't give you a tip either. I've transported passengers who do not tip when they have just saved $20 or more on event parking. They have also saved the frustration of navigating away from the event location.

I've long since stopped wondering why these passengers don't tip. Not meaning to be rude but "cheap is as cheap does" and giving the rideshare driver a tip cuts into the money saved, right? This is another example of social engineering, thinking about what most people do, when, and why.

A challenging and time-consuming approach to the pick-up location can make the hassle of transporting these passengers seem like significantly more "work" and burns earning time meaning could be less income for your time even with Surge Pricing.

Again, every driver must make the decision where to drive and when to drive for themselves, and a handful of experiences probably does not identify a statistically-significant trend.

I typically make the call based on the way I feel at the time: sometimes I feel patient, other times I do not. Driving around the end of big events can be tough.

Another thought about big events, a thought that also translates into more general social engineering thinking: If you are planning your rideshare drive to be available at the end of a big event, remember you are not the only rideshare driver thinking this way.

Sometimes the best places to drive are not the obvious places to drive. When I figured this out I became more comfortable with hanging out, for example, in the suburbs far away from "the action."

I've spent whole nights never getting close to known hot spots and ended the shift with earnings over my average of $20 an hour. I like these shifts, less traffic, less pedestrians, less stress.

And even if getting Trip Requests away from "the action" means a little less income... you guessed it - my average hourly income has always been consistent over time.

Final thoughts on the question of when to drive, I've gotten into the trap of thinking: *"right now would not be the best time to earn"* and decided to stay off the road, not get out and earn.

It took a while for me to get to get through my skull, but now I know if my earning goals for the week include putting 40 hours on the road, then over-rationalizing the best times to drive is not useful thinking.

Earnings average out over time; if I put in the hours I tend to reach my earning goals.

If I skip driving on a Tuesday night because I suspect I won't be "that busy" I'm risking ending the week with less than 40 hours and given the law of averages less than $800.

Over time you will define your own rideshare driving best practices including your best practices for "finding" your next trip, until then, and even after... go easy on yourself knowing rideshare driving is not an exact science, more of an art, and luck will always be in play.

DRIVING FOR MULTIPLE TNCs SIMULTANEOUSLY

"Expect the best. Prepare for the worst. Capitalize on what comes." - Zig Ziglar

It makes good business sense for rideshare drivers to have multiple income sources. If you only drive for one TNC a glitch in the driver application or rideshare driver paperwork issue could prevent you from driving.

This has happened to me more than once over the past two years, including missing all four days of 2016 Memorial Day weekend, easily $400-$500 income. I sat at home the entire weekend trying to get the TNC's support organization to sort out a simple paperwork mix up.

Memorial Day weekend, I planned to work 8+ hours, four days in a row: Friday, Saturday, Sunday, and Monday. I was new to rideshare driving and was only signed up with the dominate TNC in my city. This meant I had only one source of rideshare driving income.

As a new rideshare driver I had been completing trips and making money without issue for six weeks.

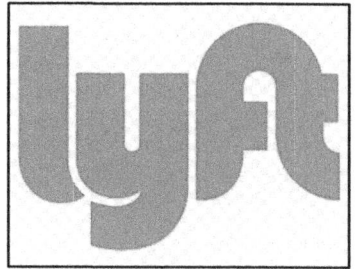

Friday at 6 p.m. I dropped my kids off for the weekend with their mom, opened the TNC application on my phone and selected "Go Online" ready to kick off a big weekend of rideshare driving.

The driver application returned a "login error." I tried everything, I deleted and reloaded TNC driver application, I restarted phone multiple times then I contacted the TNC support organization.

Despite my "heroic" efforts persistently pursuing a fix from the TNC's support organization I was not able to get the issue fixed and go online until Monday after 6 p.m.

I missed the busy weekend of earnings and had to borrow money from family to pay my rent. The very next day I started the process to sign

up with the number two TNC in my city, resolved in my thinking I would always have at least two sources of rideshare driving income.

MULTIPLE INCOME SOURCES

"*10 Reasons to Have Multiple Income Streams*" US News & World Report https://tinyurl.com/yd2hos8r

As independent contractors rideshare drivers can "work" for multiple Transportation Network Companies (TNC) simultaneously.

For a moment think of driving for Uber and Lyft as if you mowed grass for pay using your personal lawnmower. Likely you would have multiple customers with single-family homes, and you might occasionally mow grass for a landscaping company.

The landscaping company calls you when they have more work than their regular staff can complete on schedule and they pay you a negotiated price for performing a service, working as a contractor, completing specific work. The landscaping company does not deduct taxes from what they pay you, they contracted your work and you are not using their physical equipment to complete the work.

Your business is defined as: you mowing lawns with your personal lawnmower - you are independent of the lawn mowing company and can do "gigs" for another lawn mowing company, even a competitor of the first company.

As an independent contractor you don't have any traditional employee benefits and I'm arguing you don't want benefits, you want income from gigs; defined work.

You complete the defined work: "Mow this field" approaching the work the way you think the defined work should be completed and within reason, on your time schedule.

As a contractor, and not an employee, it's logical the landscape company does not control you, or have any influence over your other sources of income.

The same relationship is true for rideshare drivers working with multiple TNCs.

The dominate rideshare TNCs in the United States are Uber and Lyft. Uber is the dominate player.

As of 2018 Lyft is not in as many cities and does not have as many passengers. In a handful of U.S. cities there are other TNC players with small, but interesting, passenger market share.

These shared-economy, gig-economy transportation network companies (TNC) want you to drive for them.

Uber and Lyft must constantly bring new drivers onboard because most rideshare drivers do not stick with rideshare driving for very long. At any given time approximately two-thirds of active rideshare drivers started less than 90 days ago and at the end of one year about 90% of drivers are done, presumably will never rideshare drive again.

Likely some drivers consider themselves "active" because their paperwork is current, but they drive sporadically and only a few hours a month, or they haven't driven "In a while."

The point here: Uber and Lyft constantly need drivers and are not in a position to care if a driver is completing trips for both companies. Even if they did care there's nothing they can do unless they make drivers employees.

Uber and Lyft actually compete for the active driver's attention by designing income-boosting promotions to influence which TNC driver applications the drivers are using the most.

It's very important to Uber and Lyft's business model that drivers continue to be independent contractors and not employees. To avoid potential lawsuits Uber and Lyft have to be very careful not to appear to be treating drivers like employees in any way.

If Uber and Lyft had to treat drivers as employees in every market/city where they operated… then, without exaggeration, they are out of business, gone, the rideshare transportation "game" would be over.

NO TRASH TALK… ZERO!

Working for multiple TNCs, in the U.S. likely Uber and Lyft, it is also important to keep in mind the agreements you have with the TNC - the contract you signed to be a driver for the TNC.

In that contract there are words to the effect of: "…a driver can be disconnected from the application… for publicly criticizing…"

"Publicly criticizing the TNC."

Passengers in your car are "The Public" and don't forget this reality for a moment!

My rule: 100% professional, I do not say negative things about the companies that are my sources of income.

It may seem like common sense not to trash talk the sources of my paychecks, but I'm in my car right? These are my passengers, right? This guy/girl seems really cool and we are connecting like we've been friends for years! Where is the harm in saying what I really think?

More than once I've had passengers who asked about working for both companies and after we've been talking for a while they mentioned: "I work for Uber (or Lyft) corporate office."

The TNCs have offices in many of the cities where they operate, and the people who work in the local offices use rideshare transportation to get around.

My rule of thumb, I avoid "talking out of school," meaning anytime I'm talking about Uber or Lyft I am professional. I am a business owner, Uber and Lyft are two of my income sources.

When passengers ask: "Which one do you like better?" and they will, I answer honestly talking about how Uber controls most of the passenger market in my city, so Uber is an essential source of rides, my income.

If my passengers seem "cool" I might say: "*In my experience there are differences between the Uber and Lyft driver applications, but both companies are in the same business, and the only meaningful difference to me, as a driver, is market share, meaning rides, meaning income.*"

DAY-TO-DAY PRACTICE OF WORKING WITH UBER AND LYFT

In Denver, the top two TNCs are Uber and Lyft. When I get out on the road to earn I am usually running both Uber and Lyft driver applications simultaneously.

My passengers frequently ask about driving for both TNCs: "How does that work?"

The answer I give: *"I'm running both applications on my phone, if I get a Trip Request from Lyft then I go offline on the Uber application, essentially I am turning the other application off."*

At a surface level it really is that simple to work with Uber and Lyft at the same time.

After accepting a Trip Request my goal is to turn the other TNC application off, meaning go offline as soon as I can do so safely.

So, working for multiple TNCs simultaneously is really that simple, although it can feel complicated when you have Trip Requests coming in from Uber and Lyft at the same time. Or you accept a Trip Request with Lyft and before you can go offline with Uber you get a Trip Request on their driver application.

More than once I have seen news articles where a rideshare driver has crashed their car and blames a distraction from an incoming TNC driver application Trip Request for losing attention to watching the road.

In my opinion it is not ideal that the TNC Trip Requests, which expire in about 30 seconds, also show some details about the passenger and the pick-up location. I need reading glasses to read the details and I'm not wearing my reading glasses when I am driving.

The TNC's software sends Trip Requests to the closest driver. If that driver does not accept the request the TNC's software will automatically send the request to the next closest driver, repeating this process until a driver accepts the request.

There is a very simple way to handle receiving a Trip Request on your phone while you are driving. If you can't safely review the information displayed on the Trip Request just accept the new Trip Request before it expires, now you have to choose which trip to complete.

Don't let the stress of your "pinging" phone and an expiring-in-30-seconds Trip Request distract you from the road – "First Do No Harm!"

Just because you accepted a Trip Request does not mean you have to complete the trip. After accepting the

Trip Request, you can be safe on the road and determine if you going to pick the passenger up. If you don't want the trip, choose the "Cancel/No Charge" option.

If you cancel a Trip Request after you accepted, it will be a bit inconvenient for the potential passenger. The passenger will be notified by the TNC passenger application that the driver canceled the ride and that the passenger will not be charged. The passenger will have to re-enter their Trip Request. While this is less than ideal for passengers, crashing your car because you are distracted by a "pinging" phone is not an option.

Alternatively, you could let a new Trip Request go by without doing anything.

If you have, for example, a Lyft passenger in your car and you forgot to turn the Uber application off, you can let the new Uber Trip Request go by, don't do anything until after the Trip Request expires. After the Trip Request expires turn Uber (of Lyft) off, go offline.

taxify

When you are running multiple TNC driver applications always be safe on the road. Rideshare drivers are professional drivers and driving safely is a professional driver's #1 responsibility!

Uber, Lyft, and the other TNCs track rideshare drivers "Cancelation Rate"; "Acceptance Rate" and a few other metrics and sometimes display them to drivers in the driver applications as scores, for example "Acceptance Rate = 96%."

The TNCs track and display these metrics because human psychology experiments have shown when presented with an opportunity to "earn" a score – most human beings are motivated toward having higher scores.

Essentially every smart phone game uses this motivation principle; a "new high score" or completing another level motivates us to continue to play the game.

Your personal scores as a rideshare driver might be interesting during an active income-boosting Promotion or Bonus offer (read offer details carefully) but for all practical purposes a rideshare driver's past history for "Acceptance Rate" and "Cancellation Rate" do not directly affect a rideshare driver's ability to earn.

COO

SIDECAR

You might receive a "nastygram" or see notifications in the driver's application: "Your acceptance rate is low," but you will not be disconnected from the driver application without receiving prior warning from the TNC.

The transportation network companies need drivers to be on the road accepting Trip Requests and completing trips, it's not in their interest to cut you off without having a very good reason.

The TNCs know working toward high scores, however meaningless, "drives" rideshare driver behavior toward the TNC's goals, goals which may not be a direct match with the rideshare driver's primary goal – making money (while being safe.)

CARMA

THE NOT SO FUN STUFF...

"Tough times never last, but tough people do."   ~Robert H. Schuller

KNOW WHEN TO SAY "NO" – Part One

After about six months of rideshare driving I gave myself permission to take control of my rideshare driving days; I gave myself permission to just say: "No" to some passengers, before I let them into my car.

It took some time, sometimes I can be a little dense before the lightbulb comes on.

After about six months of rideshare driving I realized the TNC driver application "Cancel/No Charge" option has the power to all but eliminate some of the negative aspects of the rideshare driving "job."

The best way to describe the change in my thinking: I realized I did not have to transport people who did not treat me and my car in a respectful manner. Before making this important mental shift, when "bad" things happened I tried to "grin and bear it", as result I 'suffered' through subtle and not-so-subtle rude passenger behavior.

When I made this mental switch, realizing that I did not have to complete every Trip Request I accepted, I felt powerful and more in charge of my experiences. The stress I sometimes felt while driving, or at home thinking about getting out to drive, was dramatically reduced.

By formalizing and clearly defining my personal rideshare driving rules, the stress of anticipating the possibility of future "bad" passengers was almost eliminated.

In most traditional working-with-the-public jobs, there is a manager or supervisor to call when things "Go South." Line employees do not have to suffer through customer "abuse" and only managers and supervisors can make exceptions for customers.

As a rideshare driver you are the manager and you get to decide when to say: "No."

There are two situations listed below where I will always say "no" to the trip.

In both cases I have to say: "No" when face-to-face with potential passengers:

1. **I will never transport anyone after they have attempted to overload my car with extra passengers.**

   Legally you can only transport as many passengers as you have available seatbelts, and if you are breaking this law you will not be covered by any insurance policy, so if something happens, guess who's on-the-hook?

   During my first few months as a driver, I overloaded my car with passengers a couple of times, each time I drove away questioning if I should have accepted the ride.

   I felt like the passengers were taking advantage of me, as a rideshare driver, and was also concerned I was putting excessive wear on my car and even risking breaking something I will have to pay to repair. The TNCs will not pay for damage that happened when a rideshare driver has overloaded their car.

   In my life I've never liked saying: "No", especially when I am face-to-face with another human being.

   And in my life, I have usually tried to explain or justify my actions, said something to explain why I was saying: "No."

   Before I made my personal rule to always say: "No" when asked to overload my car, I responded to a Trip Request in Boulder, CO and at the pick-up location was asked to transport five passengers. I explained that I could not because it would be against the law and mean I was driving with no insurance coverage. We renegotiated and I took three of the five, the other two waited for another rideshare driver.

The trip seemed to go fine, we talked a little, I apologized I could not take them all in the same ride even offered to return for the other two passengers.

I was polite and professional at all times, including the conversation at the pick-up location where we renegotiated the trip to transport three of the five passengers.

After the ride, the passenger who called the ride gave me a one-star rating and wrote a negative review to Uber; including suggesting I was unfit to be an Uber driver and that I should be fired!

Obviously, I was not "fired," just notified that a passenger was unhappy with my actions.

Rideshare drivers are not fired… in some cases they are suspended from having access to the TNC driver application. Suspensions might be a day or two; a week; a month; or in extreme cases a lifetime suspension.

Please don't worry your TNC driver application access will be suspended because I customer lied about your behavior. Before the TNC support organization resources suspend a driver from the application they will evaluate the customer's report and will communicate with the driver.

I believe the driver's trip history/customer history will also be evaluated by support resources; it's unlikely a high-rated driver with dozens of positive reviews will suddenly go "off the deep end" on a single trip?

If you still have any concern, remember this too: The TNCs are currently desperate for drivers due to the high attrition rate for new drivers. The TNCs know most drivers will not stick with the gig for more than three months and only 10% of drivers are still accepting and completing trips one year after starting.

It is not in the TNC's business interests to suspend active drivers. A notable exception, if a customer reports a driver was under the influence of drugs or alcohol. If this happens the driver's access to the application will probably be immediately suspended and TNC support will call the driver to confirm the report.

As I've said before, I don't worry much about my TNC driver average star rating, but I did not like having a one-star rating on my Uber driver profile until another 500 passengers bothered to rate me as a driver.

With Uber a driver's average star rating reflect their most recent 500 rated trips. Passengers are not required to rate drivers and historically less than half of my passengers bother to give me a rating.

During the months it took to rotate that one-star rating off my average star rating, I considered asking my passengers to rate me to speed up the process, I never did because I don't want to have potentially negative-feeling interactions during my workday.

If I asked passengers to rate me I would have to talk about the incident and probably explain the "nuts and bolts" details of how the star rating systems work, no thank you.

Important to mention, my Uber star rating with the one-star included was 4.89 out of 5 stars.

Looking back now at that experience what was I thinking? Why was I spending any energy concerned about a 4.89 star rating and more importantly why was I willing to renegotiate with potential passengers expecting me to do something illegal?

I SAY NO

After saying "No" to an unreasonable passenger's request it's not logical to expect a five-star rating and a generous tip?

I shouldn't have been surprised when I received a one-star rating; no tip; and blatant lies about me in the passenger's written comments to the TNC.

Seriously: What was I thinking?!!!

Rideshare passengers requesting you overload your vehicle are only interested in saving money, they do not respect the shared-economy nature of rideshare transportation. The idea of a shared-economy is people are respectfully sharing resources in a mutually-beneficial way.

When a potential passenger, or a passenger in your car, is making an unreasonable request, it is not logical to believe they are going to tip you for accommodating their request or even respect your professionalism for politely refusing to, in this example, break the law by overloading your car with passengers.

A few times I tried to explain why I wouldn't overload my car, in response I heard things like:

"We don't mind, we'll squeeze in" or *"One of us will duck down so the police will not see them"* or *"Do it for us, just this once."*

Over time passenger's responses to my professional approach to rideshare driving helped me learn that after I make a decision and say "No" there is: "Nothing to discuss."

I know I'm repeating but I believe the phrase: "Nothing to discuss" is a powerful tool for rideshare drivers.

Easily 99% of the trips a rideshare driver completes do not require <u>any</u> detailed discussion, it is not logical to have discussions about exception requests which could be anything.

Trying to find the "right" thing to say in every situation would be difficult. I figured this out while sitting on my couch trying to talk myself into getting out on the road to earn.

In my experience the "mental game" of being a rideshare driver has the potential to spoil the whole rideshare driving gig.

More than once I've been surprised at the things that have been said to me at the pick-up location by prospective passengers and while they are still outside my car.

In these brief interactions, brief because of my approach, I often drive away thinking:

"Why does someone who has all but yelled at me even want to get into my car if my 'No' became a 'Yes?' Are they really so driven to have their way they would be willing to get into my car and trust their safety to my driving after chewing me out?"

My best answer, to behave this way people must be thinking rideshare drivers are employees of the TNC, at least unconsciously because they haven't fully thought through how rideshare transportation works.

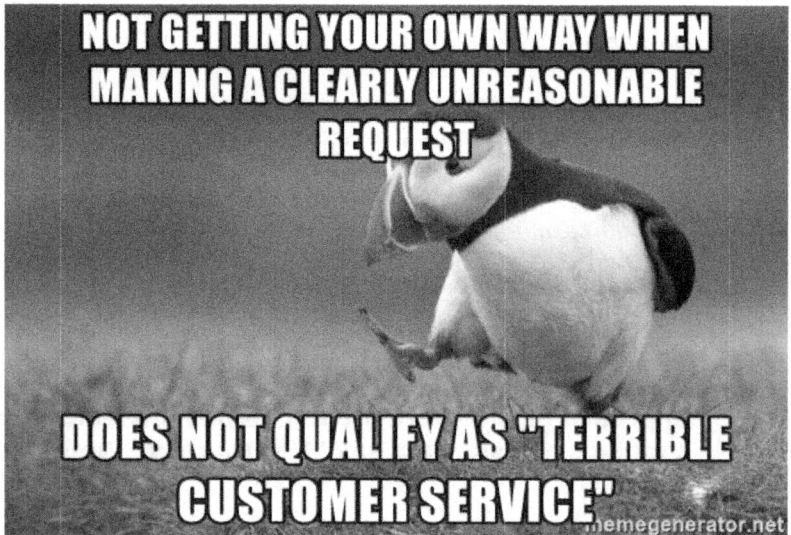

NOT GETTING YOUR OWN WAY WHEN MAKING A CLEARLY UNREASONABLE REQUEST

DOES NOT QUALIFY AS "TERRIBLE CUSTOMER SERVICE"

When addressing someone as if they were an employee supervised by a higher power some people will behave as if employees are required to endure a little abuse from customers.

I'm always open to learning new ways of conducting myself, in fact every rideshare driving day I am learning and practicing how to be the kind of rideshare driver I want to be.

But, I am not an employee, I run a business, I am the boss.

The TNC driver applications connect me to my customers by sending me Trip Requests, and "requests" is the key word here. I do not have to complete every Trip Request I accept.

Just in case, I would never say: *"My business, I am the boss"* to a potential passenger.

I'm talking about an internal mindset that helps me make decisions on the rare occurrences when there is an exception to the normally routine task of picking up passengers and safely transporting them from Point A to Point B.

When the people I have encountered as a rideshare driver aren't getting their way, the details of why I said: "No" never seemed to matter. These **passengers didn't care why I said: "No"**, they just wanted what they wanted and apparently thought it was a reasonable request.

I like to remind myself that these requests might very well have been accommodated on the passenger's past trips, new drivers are more easily manipulated by passengers who are willing to push the limits.

I'd like to believe I'm doing rideshare "the right way" but since every driver gets to choose how to run their own rideshare driving business there are as many "right" ways to do the gig as there are rideshare drivers on the road.

Passengers who want to, as example, overload my car are communicating loudly... communicating with their actions they do not respect rideshare drivers and their personal cars.

Remember, the exception requests are not personal, these potential passengers did not look at your driver profile photo and think: "We could probably take advantage of this guy." They were planning to, as example, overload any rideshare car that showed up.

I'm not ok with being treated in a disrespectful manner I hope you feel the same.

Don't get mad; don't spend energy on a pointless conversation with a stranger; just make a choice in your mind, then take action; a brief interaction where you control the conversation, I suggest saying:

"I've canceled the ride and you will not be charged" and as needed *"There is nothing to discuss."*

Have the brief interaction then move on with your day, happier and less stressed.

When I first started rideshare driving it could take hours or even days to shake off a negative interaction that happened during my rideshare driving day.

Now I am able to shake off negative events fairly quickly. I do allow myself to say my negative thoughts out loud, but only when I'm the only one in the car, for example I might say out loud:

"It escapes me why pedestrians are not run over more often?!!!"

If an experience sticks with me, I might share the experience with one of my next rides, although I'm not going to force the story on any passenger just because they were my next passenger.

My goal when talking about the experience is to laugh it off: *"You won't believe just happened to me."* A talkative passenger can help me shake off the experience that shook me up, so I can go on with my day, neutral in my thinking, and focused on making money.

2. **The other situation where I always say "No" to a trip is when I am asked to take a solo passenger home who is obviously extremely drunk.**

When I first started driving there were a couple of occasions where I allowed someone who was not getting in the car to say: *"Please get my friend home safely..."* then I drove the drunk home. More than once I've helped an inebriated passenger to their door.

At first these experiences did not bother me much, I even thought I was doing a good deed. Over time these experiences helped me create my second rideshare driving business: "Unbreakable Rule."

Months after I made this unbreakable rule, I said "No" when I was asked to get a 20-something female home safely after I had watched her unable to walk down a sidewalk on her own.

The "request" was phrased as a direction, like my boss telling me something I was going to do: "Hi, you're going to take our friend home."

I'm thinking:

"Uhhh yeah… telling me what I'm going to do instead of asking if I would be willing to… very unlikely to result in me saying sure, no problem"

The young woman they wanted me to drive home as a solo passenger had fallen-down making her way to my car multiple times, despite having two people, one on each side, trying to hold her up as she stumbled/walked down the sidewalk.

This unbreakable rule is easy for me to enforce, I am very clear in my mind that helping someone to their door and tucking them into bed is simply not part of the service I am willing to provide.

If you think about it, I suspect neither are you, and if you are hesitating even a little while thinking about this situation, consider the fact that this an incredibly unreasonable request opens you up to potential liability. The next day the drunk person and/or the person who poured the drunk into your car can say anything about you.

It doesn't matter if what they say is the truth or not. You will have to defend your actions, what really happened. I'd rather defend the fact that I said "No" and did not pick someone up, did not transporting them anywhere; compared to defending myself when presented with complicated lies, after all I have no witnesses, it's just me out there, alone.

In the example with the 20-something female, as I said the woman didn't even ask by saying: *"Will you get my friend home safely..."* She told me: *"You will be getting my friend home safely."*

And after I said "No" she argued with me, speaking very forcefully:

"Isn't it is part of your job to make sure people get home safely?!!!"

After I repeated that I was not going to transport her friend, the person making the "request" started yelling at me as if she were my boss, and an extremely bad boss.

She leaned her upper body into my front passenger window, I assume trying to get in my face. She cursed at me; told me I
was a bad person; and promised to *"Call Uber tomorrow and get me fired."*

To get her out of my car I had to say:

"The next thing I am going to do is call 911 and get the police involved, is that what you want?"

A young man watching the interaction grabbed her by the waist and physically pulled her out of my front seat passenger window then I drove away.

In my rideshare driving experiences, over 11,000 trips, I've been cursed at more than once; honked at countless times; once been asked: "Are you out of your mind?" when I refused to let someone in my car; and at least three times been threatened by potential passengers to: "Have me fired."

When I flipped the mental switch, to take control of my rideshare driving days; mostly by mentally preparing myself to say "No" to potential passenger, say "No" with zero second-guessing; when I flipped that mental switch, almost all of my negative thinking about earning all of my income as a rideshare driver was gone.

The most common time for potential passengers to curse at me is when I've said:

"I have canceled the ride, you will not be charged, you can call another driver."

I see the cursing as confirmation I made the correct decision, if a passenger is willing to curse at a stranger for saying "No" to their unreasonable request, if I had let them in my car it is unlikely it would have been a pleasant trip for me.

Depending on how I feel at the time, I might make exceptions, after all it's always up to me right?

I might offer to accept the falling-down-drunk trip if someone accompanies the inebriated person home. I might even offer to wait and bring the "babysitter" back to the party.

On the other hand, a falling down drunk is also a vomit risk, even with a babysitter to hold up my gallon-sized, zip-lock carsick bag.

I suspect the best practice, for me and other rideshare drivers, is probably just saying: "No" to vomit-risk passengers, that is if they are identifiable before they enter the car.

I've never ejected someone as a vomit-risk after we have started to drive; but I have talked about not wanting someone throwing up in the car; told passengers to "say the word" and I will pull over to the curb immediately; and passed out my "Just in case" gallon-sized zip-lock carsick bags.

If someone does get sick in a rideshare vehicle, the TNC will reimburse the driver for cleaning costs up to $250; but the TNC is not going to pay the driver anything for the time lost until the vehicle is ready to rideshare drive again.

You can't transport passengers in a car that smells like vomit, and of course there is the unpleasant task of dealing with the mess. The one time it has happened to me, I had the inside of my car professionally detailed the next day. I even asked the shop to remove the backseat and insure that all traces of the incident were removed.

If you say "No" to any part of a passenger's requests, it is unlikely you will get a favorable star rating, and obviously you are not going to get a generous tip or any tip at all. Remember, if you never choose "Start Trip" instead choose the "Cancel/No Charge" option, passengers cannot give you a star rating, and without a completed financial transaction they will have to work to contact the TNC support organization to complain about you.

Consider this, if someone is falling-down drunk they are breaking the law the moment they step out of a private home into the public domain – a law-enforcement officer could charge them for "public intoxication."

Saying "No" to these trips is not about you failing to: "Get them home safely." This person was already behaving irresponsibly to get into this condition, and they are already breaking the law by being in a public place where you can pick them up in your car.

I suggest you say "No" to falling-down drunks as solo passengers.

I suggest you just say: "No" and in your mind let the experience go.

Drive away knowing it's not your problem to solve.

Final thoughts on this one: you will be, at least occasionally, transporting people who have been drinking alcohol and sometimes it will show in their behavior. Most people can handle a few alcoholic beverages and not be a total bonehead in a rideshare driver's car.

In this section I'm not talking about people who have just been drinking alcohol, I'm talking about a "falling-down-drunk"; someone unable who is unable to "watch" after themselves.

Even if the falling-down-drunk is capable of stumbling to your car and then capable of getting into your car by themselves, it does not mean they will be able to get out of your car unassisted when you reach the drop-off location.

With this unbreakable rule, I'm saying it's not my job to transport falling-down drunks anywhere; and my response to these requests, saying: "No" to the trip, is not personal, it is based on an unbreakable rule of my business.

Also, not personal because it was luck that put me in the situation, I just happened to be the closest driver when the Trip Request was entered into the TNC passenger application.

Repeating myself because the point is so important:

> If you choose to take a "falling-down-drunk" passenger home, and they are the only passenger in your car, the next morning the passenger, and/or the person who asked you to "babysit" the passenger, can say anything about you and say anything about what happened during the trip and even after the trip was completed.

Saying "anything" includes saying that you broke the law, for example with unwanted physical touch... I don't want to ever be in this position, a really good reason this is one of my unbreakable rules for my rideshare driving business.

As a boy my Mom taught me: "To avoid being accused of doing something wrong, the best tactic is to do not knowingly get into a situation where someone can tell lies about your behavior." Thanks Mom, you are the best!

UNDERAGE PASSENGERS

TNCs (Uber, Lyft, Taxify, etc.) have a rule that rideshare passengers must be at least 18 years old to travel without an adult in the car. This rule mitigates the TNC's liability with regard to underage customers traveling without an adult in the car. Underage Americans, less than 18 years old, cannot enter legally-binding contracts.

As a rideshare driver I don't ask passengers for IDs and I have also refused passengers at the curb who are obviously underage, saying: *"You must be 18 years old when using this service."*

How drivers screen passengers at the curb is entirely up to the individual driver.

Bear in mind if you are bending or breaking the TNC's published rules you are probably taking a liability risk. If something happens while underage passengers are in your car the TNC's insurance company (likely your personal insurance company too) will be looking for reasons to deny the claim.

If there are issues when an underage passenger is traveling in a rideshare driver's car they could be suspended from having access to the TNC's driver application.

While the liability question is primarily related to vehicle insurance, there is also the liability of being responsible for an underage individual; the safest practice is to never take an unnecessary risk – "First do no harm."

The question of underage passengers is an example of how the TNCs expect rideshare drivers to enforce the TNC's published rules.

This is neither good or bad, some passengers won't know the TNC's rules, and some passengers do know and will try to get drivers to bend or break the rules.

The nature of rideshare transportation means drivers will have some potentially difficult conversations with people using the TNC passenger applications.

Rather than get frustrated by this reality, I prefer to think of it as part of the rideshare driving gig. Yes, it can be annoying but rideshare driving is a choice; I choose to drive.

RUDE PASSENGERS

Passengers will sometimes behave rudely, or at least do something that feels rude to me.

Most drivers will consider a long wait at the pick-up location rude, especially when the pick-up location required a significant amount of time to reach, or is in a busy downtown area where it can be difficult to find a safe place to wait, out of traffic flow.

It feels like rude passenger behavior when I've driven more than a few minutes to reach the pick-up location, the TNCs tell passengers to

be ready to go before they request a ride, when a driver accepts the Trip Request the passenger is notified: "Your driver will arrive in 8 minutes." If after driving 8 minutes to the pick-up location I'm left waiting minutes at the curb... then the passenger wasn't ready to go and shouldn't have requested a ride? Rude!

Sometimes, I feel like passenger's questions are too personal; however, questions that feel too personal to me, might not feel too personal to other drivers. Every passenger and every driver is different, what bugs me might not bug you at all.

When a passenger seems to be behaving rudely I suggest not reacting or reacting as little as possible. If I feel "bugged" by a passenger I typically look at the GPS application map and think: "5 more minutes and you are out of my car."

When I'm feeling bored or just wanting to disconnect from the current passenger in my car, I like to focus on the music playing, singing the words to myself, just in my head, or just mouthing the words.

COMMON PASSENGER TYPES

In a college psychology course, the professor said:

"*Stereotypes exist because there is at least a kernel of truth in what the stereotype suggests.*"

The professor's point was stereotypes can be useful when they do not prevent us from giving people the opportunity to show who they are with their behavior; they might live up to the stereotype or they might surprise us.

So, with the goal of preparing you for some of the common types of passengers I have created a few rideshare passenger stereotypes. It's not my intent to make fun of anyone, again my goal is helping you be a successful rideshare driver.

- **The Distractor** – these passengers seem oblivious to the reality that driving requires 100% focus on the road. Often their distractions will look like a lot of questions (See "The Inquisitor" below) but I've had passengers trying to show me things on their phone while I'm driving and do all kinds of things likely to surprise you as a new rideshare driver.
  - After 11,000 trips I am rarely surprised anymore but I would never agree I have "seen it all" because I see new things all the time... there are an unlimited supply of human beings in the world and we are all different.

Distractors may ask you to play specific kinds of music or play a very specific song; and they will probably make the request while you are busy driving.

After you start driving Distractors sometimes ask if you know of a gas station or convenience store is located which is also on the way to their drop-off location. It has never been my goal to have encyclopedic knowledge of every part of the city and it never will be.

- o The passenger has a smart phone so could look up the answer themselves? We know they have a smart phone or they wouldn't have been able to request the trip in the first place.
- o Certainly, no harm in passengers asking, I may know the answer, or I may say we can watch for one or ask them if they have one in mind on the way to where they are going. If I think I can do so safely I might even look up the request in my map program but I always remember my "job" is doing the driving safely, I pay attention to the road!

The worst thing Distractors do is start being distracting from the moment they get into the car, often making it difficult for me to confirm I have the correct passenger (correct name on the Trip Request) and the correct drop-off location.

Distractors can make it challenging to think about where you are going and how you will get there and, in my experience, might act surprised that you are not able to do multiple things at the same time while also transporting them safely to their destination.

At the start of trips, I sometimes interrupt The Distractor and say: *"Let's get the paperwork done first…"* then I confirm passenger name and drop-off location all before I have moved my car from the pick-up location.

- o You control when the car moves and not moving can be a powerful communication.
- o Breaking The Distractor's behavior by interrupting them can also be a powerful communication. You are in charge of how the ride goes, be polite but act like you are in charge and most passengers will respect you and behave respectfully.

- **The Inquisitor** – these passengers are often distractors too and will ask questions... lots of them.

Often the questions begin immediately, even before they close the car door. Often, the questions are about the nature of being a rideshare driver, but they can be on almost any subject including ones you may find a bit personal.

  - More than once an Inquisitor has said: "*I ask these questions of all my drivers!*" I'm thinking: "*Lucky me*" but I don't say it out loud.
  - Imagine how a professional taxi driver might respond if a passenger entered their car and said: "*I ask all my taxi drivers these questions...*" Hard to imagine a traditional taxi driver responding politely? Now that's funny right there, I don't care who you are...

At a TNC driver's event a female rideshare driver told me: "*When the conversation starts going in a direction I don't want to go... I just change the subject. I do not say 'I don't want to talk about that' or 'that question is too personal' or 'your subtle sexual references are inappropriate.' I just change the subject, start talking about something else.*"

I whole-heartedly agree with her, I work very hard to not say things to my passengers likely to create an uncomfortable situation.

  - Not responding can be a powerful tool as well, human beings are typically uncomfortable when they do not know what to think about the current situation.
  - If you don't say anything they have to guess what you are thinking, and this will create at least a break while they ponder what to say next.

- **The Next-Door Neighbor** – These passengers more than hold up their end of the conversation and talk about all kinds of things. The Next-Door Neighbor might ask questions about rideshare driving but they will be very respectful in the manner they ask and will often say: "*If you don't mind me asking.*"

I have had some of the best conversations of my life and some of the most thought-provoking, and sometimes deeply spiritual (not religious) conversations of my life with strangers, my rideshare passengers.

- **The Substitute Teacher's Tormentor** - Seems like I got this kind of passenger more often when I was a new driver, a "rookie." Their behavior is hard to generalize but they are usually pretty blatantly trying to "Get your goat" in any way you can imagine and in ways you never would have imagined until they happen to you.

    I still get Tormentors, but I think my skin is a lot thicker now, and since I'm unlikely to react to what they say I'm not much fun to torment and the behavior tends to die out pretty quickly.
    - Sometime Tormentors bend the stereotype because what they say is spirited but also respectful and intelligent; they don't sound like a drunk guy heckling the comedian.
    - Sometimes the things the Tormentor says has broken my stereotype, perhaps because what they say displays a better than average intellect. In those cases, I often have fun, roll out my best witty responses, and often these trips give me big belly laughs. Laughing is healthy, and I laugh a lot while I'm rideshare driving.

I also believe after hosting over fifteen-thousand different human beings in my car I am more relaxed now compared to when I first started rideshare driving; because I am relaxed I don't come off like a new driver and am less likely to bring out Substitute Teacher Tormentor behavior in my passengers.

Remember sometimes the most powerful thing you can say is: Nothing.

Sometimes I think situation comedies on television make me think I should have something clever to say in any situation, this is my ego talking, as a rideshare driver saying nothing will serve you well, anything important your passenger says will be repeated if they think it is necessary.

I have broken the say nothing rule thinking I needed to say something very direct.

As example, I had a passenger once echoing my professional answers to her unreasonable requests, only in her echo of my response she would add: *"Oh he say f$$k that..."*

- o After she did this three times I said: *"Excuse me, I have not used the work f$$k once so please stop putting that word in my mouth."*

- o When I spoke up we were less than two minutes from the drop-off location and I had already decided to give her a three-star rating so the TNC application would never match us again.

- o She was being not only behaving rudely but, in my opinion, verbally attacking me on a personal level, as a rule I do not use profanity, if I use a curse word I am one step away from going nuclear something I never want to do while I am rideshare driving.

This is an unusual story for me. Unusual in part because this passenger was persistently rude, I ignored her rude behavior for over five minutes.

Unusual as well because I stick to the rideshare behavior guidelines written in this book pretty faithfully, I didn't need to "train" this woman to not be rude to rideshare drivers and I wasn't feeling neutral, in my mind I judged this woman's behavior as "bad."

Most importantly I didn't keep my "eyes on the prize" and stay focused on the fact that this ride was another "fish" for the "big green basket" of money I will be taking home at the end of the day.

I could have stopped my thinking at: "Don't want this passenger in my car again so I will rate her three stars or less."

- • **The Confessor** – In my twenties I worked as a bartender including bartending gigs where I had customers sitting at my bar for hours. Bartender can't "escape" customers as easily a waiter who can walk away from a customer's table; a bartender is trapped behind the bar and the rideshare driver is in a similar situation.

Some rideshare passengers talk to me as if I were their therapist and sometimes they share very personal details about their lives, it surprised me at first but now I know reasons why it makes some sense to share personal things about yourself to a rideshare driver.

- o The rideshare experience is almost completely anonymous. You and your passengers are strangers; strangers who will be spending a short time in very close quarters.
- o The likelihood of getting the same driver (or passenger) a second time is pretty remote. People have shared intimate stories about their lives in my car. I try to listen and not give advice. I figure The Confessors just want to talk so I let them.

A customer sitting at a bar might be holding back because they don't want to be too embarrassed to come back another day. With this in mind it makes sense the anonymous nature of rideshare transportation will lead some people to share. Just listen and if you become uncomfortable the ride will not last forever.

Of course if the Confessor's confessions make you uncomfortable, violent or sexual in nature say something to show you are in charge, the simplest thing to say might be: "*I don't want to talk about violent things.*"

Whatever you say don't feel the need to explain yourself and I mean don't try to explain yourself at all. The answer to "why" is simple, your car, your rules but you don't have to say that unless a passenger is being persistent.

Keep your car "clean" from negativity, neutral is what we are going for, when this ride is over you will be picking up your next passenger you don't want to be trying to get over what happened on your last ride.

- **The "Fun" Guy/Girl** – these passengers are typically loud and probably have been drinking alcohol.

They greet you boisterously while standing on the curb or as they are getting into the car with something like; "Hey brother, how are you doing tonight!!!"
  - o I have two biological brothers and at least five "brothers from a different mother." There is something

about a stranger calling me "Brother" that seems forced and insincere, but that's me not necessarily you.

- o It's like people who are not from the United Kingdom saying: "Cheers" for goodbye, if you grew up saying "Cheers" meaning "Goodbye" fine, otherwise it just sounds like you are trying too hard to sound cool.

When I first started driving I assumed The Fun Guy/Girl was communicating a desire for a jovial driver and I would try to match their enthusiasm.

Now I stay neutral and if anything, I respond in a more sedate manner. I don't want to encourage overly boisterous passengers because they are already over the "limit" for the kind of people I would prefer to transport.

The Fun/Girls can be distracting from driving safely and frankly, sometimes transporting overly-boisterous passenger is just a pain in the backside.

- **The Entitled Passenger** – this is my least favorite type of passenger.

The easiest way to describe them is they behave in a variety of ways, often very subtle, that suggest to me they believe the TNC trip pays for more than just a ride from Point A to Point B.

- o The Entitled passenger makes me feel like they think that the "own" me and my car during the trip, like a private limo ride that only costs a few bucks.

- o These passengers often want to sit in the front seat "*I always sit in the front seat.*"

- o They often show up late for the pick-up and walk very slowly to the car.

- o They might be overly friendly in a manner that makes me feel like I'm being "talked down to"; like they see me as "the help" or other subtle behaviors which make me feel I'm not being treated in a respectful manner.

Another common Entitled Passenger behavior is an unspoken expectation for the driver to "perform" for them.

- o   To be fair, about two-thirds of rideshare drivers have been on the road less than 90 days and "thanks" to the TNC online trainings on live onboarding events these new drivers mistakenly think "performing" is part of the rideshare driver gig.

- o   It's normal and natural for rideshare passengers to build their expectations about rideshare based on the type of drivers they have had in the past.

- o   In the Entitled Passenger's past rides they may have had drivers trying too hard to please or get the idea that most rideshare drivers are new so don't deserve the same respect as a seasoned driver.

- o   I confess I am likely to say things like: *"I've been doing this for almost three years and have over 11,000 lifetime trips."*

    I rationalize to myself I'm saying this to give my passengers confidence in my abilities or to make it clear I'm not new so don't expect me to be like most of your past drivers. I know the reality is this is my ego talking, I'm still working on ego reduction, I fear it will be a lifetime pursuit however being a rideshare driver gives me opportunities for practice.

Entitled Passengers can be extremely mentally and emotionally taxing making the Entitled Passenger's trips seem much longer than they really are.

- **The Wild Bunch** – similar to the the "Fun Guy/Girl" passengers only traveling in groups of 3-4 passengers.

Typically, Wild Bunches have been drinking alcohol and usually are talking very loudly as they get into the car and continue to talk loudly, even yelling, after they get into the car. I know most of us talk a little louder when we have been drinking alcohol, but I have access to the music volume on my steering wheel, the music in my car is never loud enough to require yelling to be heard.

I've had some big belly laughs with Wild Bunch passengers but if I'm tired, working on hour 8 of a 10-hour day of rideshare driving, transporting Wild Bunch passengers can feel like too much work.

With Wild Bunch trips I'm often just quiet letting them have their fun with each other as long as they are not being disrespectful to me or my car.

- o I can remember when I was younger going out with my buddies and having fun all night long; we didn't stop having fun just because we caught a taxi; we didn't care what the taxi driver thought about us because we were with the people we enjoy, and we were enjoying our lives.

- o I hope we weren't too disrespectful to taxi drivers or others and I'm certain we thought we were fun to be around. In two years of rideshare driving I've learned that if I'm drinking alcohol, drunks can be funny; when I'm sober... not so much.

If I thought about stereotypes at bit more I'm certain I could come up with a few more but the point of this section is to prepare you for the variety of passengers who will travel in your car.

In general, I do not suggest behaving differently dependent on the types of passenger in your car. My advice is the same for all passengers: be yourself; know your boundaries and enforce them only when you believe it is really necessary to "draw a line."

You can always look down at the GPS navigation screen and think: "5 more minutes and these passengers will be out of my car.

I did not feel prepared for the variety of passengers I would get when I first started rideshare driving and it was, at least at time, mentally distracting to be worrying about what kind of passengers I would get next.

When I was a new driver I spent months not enjoying the "job" and there were lots of times I had to force myself to get out and drive. **Think about that for a second: "I had to force myself"** primarily because I was worried about the types of passengers I would get.

I had to force myself to get out and make what is arguable pretty "easy" money and I didn't have another source of income. Imagine how easy it could be to avoid getting on the road for any number of reasons if you see your rideshare driving income as "extra" money?

Don't worry about the next passengers, be yourself, know your boundaries but mostly don't react to "bad" situations... keep it simple and you will do fine.

The TNC's online trainings and email updates seem to convey that every passenger will be respectful and a joy to spend time with, this will be true most of the time.

I love the stories the TNCs tell that talk about extraordinary passengers, I'm sure these stories are true but remember, hundreds of people with psychology experience, training, and backgrounds work for the TNCs... I think it pays for rideshare drivers to be a little suspicious, actually I think it pays for all human beings to be a little suspicious.

In his book: **The Five Agreements** Don Miguel Ruiz says it very well:

"Listen, but be skeptical."

In summary of this section I'd guess that 99% of my passengers do not "rub me wrong" and do not seem as though they are trying

The Five Agreements

- Be Impeccable with Your Word

- Take Nothing Personally

- Make No Assumptions

- Always Do Your Best

- Be Sceptical – but Learn to Listen

to "get my goat." Most rideshare passengers are just people trying to get somewhere.

The TNC's online trainings and customer support resources **do not** seem to provide solid advice what to do when passengers are not respectful. At least once I have pressed the point aggressively in a back and forth email exchange with a TNC's support organization, the best advice I've seen is not that great: "Decide if you want to have a given passenger in your car before you unlock your doors." Most passengers look pretty normal when they are standing at the curb waiting or when they are walking up to your car.

Remember your ride, you are in charge, your rules, and go easy on yourself.

Last thought related to working with passengers; while having a conversation with a passenger in the front seat I do not try to look at them, make eye contact, I watch the road.

Passengers can be distracting even when they are not doing "bad" things, I never take my eyes of the road when my car is moving… never!

KNOW WHEN TO SAY "NO" – Part Two

There are other reasons I will say "No" using the "Cancel/No Charge" option found in the TNC driver application, probably a pull-down option on Trip Request screen. (Sorry can't be specific, the TNCs update their applications all the time, things change.)

Some people will communicate with their actions, before they get into my car, what kind of rideshare passenger they will be, and if I think they have unreasonable expectations of what to expect from rideshare transportation they are not getting into my car.

When I have had specific examples, "bad" rideshare trips, I have pressed this point with Uber and Lyft support on multiple occasions and the best answer I've received is: "Screen passengers before you let them into your car." At the time I thought: "Not very helpful, most people look fine while standing on the curb or walking up to my car."

Over time I realized this TNC support response could be extremely helpful to me and I took it as a confirmation from the TNCs that it is ok to screen passengers before they get into the car and ok to refuse a passenger's ride when there are blatant signs they would not be respectful passengers.

As example, a potential passenger walks up to my car holding a slice of pizza, no box or napkins, doesn't come to my open passenger window to ask me if it's ok to eat in my car – just pulls on the door handle.

I had locked the doors when I saw her approaching thinking: *"Seriously, you think you're going to eat that in my car without even asking if it's ok?"*

The potential passenger came to the open car window after pulling on the door handle twice, this is very common, if the doors are locked most passengers seem to think I simple forgot to unlock the door for them.

It still bothers me a little that a locked door doesn't prompt a passenger to look into my open window and say: "*Hi I'm John, are you Wylee?*" I spent a couple of months making people confirm their name before I unlocked the doors, when I stopped doing this I was thinking I didn't want to do things that most drivers were not doing unless I believed it was really important.

So, Slice-Of-Pizza approaches my open passenger window and I say: "*You cannot eat that slice of pizza in my car.*"

She responds: "*Will you wait here while I finish it?*"

Seriously! The slice had one or two bites taken out and it was very large slice with a thick crust.

I said: "*I have canceled this trip and you will not be charged. You can call another driver*" then I drove away.

I have a handful of phrases I use over and over, like: "*I have canceled this trip and you will not be charged*" and "*There is nothing to discuss.*"

I don't try to respond to every situation on the fly, it would be too easy to say something with the potential to escalate an already negative interaction.

I've seen this kind of potential passenger behavior only a handful of times in over 11,000 lifetime trips so this kind of situation is statistically rare, but it can happen to any rideshare driver and at any time.

Hard to believe someone would expect to bring a slice of pizza, or an open drink cup, presumably containing an alcoholic beverage, on a taxi ride; but rideshare transportation is new and since two-thirds of rideshare drivers have been on the road less than 90 days these passengers may have successfully taken advantage of drivers in the past.

If a passenger gets their way once it is easy to imagine they will try again on future rides.

A new driver might not be prepared what to do in this kind of situation. For an almost unbelievable example of unreasonable passenger expectations see the Ice Cream Cone Man example on the next page.

Sometimes I give the reason why I've canceled a passenger's trip, but usually I do not. In these situations, I will always tell the potential passenger that they will not be charged, I'm a professional and I always try to behave in a professional manner.

> Recent example of saying "No" at the pickup point. There were three passengers to be picked up at the local mall and one of them had a half-eaten ice cream cone with ice cream dripping down the sides. I immediately locked my doors and told the Ice Cream Man that he could not eat an ice cream cone in my car and that I had canceled the ride and there would be no charge. Well he wanted to throw away the ice cream and still get in the car. I repeated "You will not be charged" and drove away.

Hopefully the passengers I refuse at the curb will figure out why I did not allow them in my car, but if they don't... I just do not see it as my job to "train" passengers for their future rides.

In my opinion some of the people who do these kinds of things are counting on getting their way because it's difficult for most people to say "No" to someone when face-to-face.

The rest of them, I guess they aren't using their brains, rideshare transportation is new to most people and TNC marketing tends to present unrealistic pictures of a few clicks on the application and a car magically comes to pick you up wherever you are and whatever you are doing. The driver will greet you with a big smile and accommodate if not anticipate your every need.

On more than one occasion I have canceled rides without explanation when I've seen someone walking to my car with large red Solo cups filled with an unknown beverage. I didn't give a reason because I'm not interested in seeing how that conversation would go.

What if I said:

"*It's against the law to have an open alcoholic beverage in a moving vehicle.*"

The potential passenger might say:

"*It's not alcohol it's a protein drink.*"

Then do I say:

"*I don't want your drink spilled on my seats and carpet.*"

If I were going to say that, it should have been the first thing I said? Doesn't matter to me what's in the cup I don't want it spilled in my car?

What if the potential passenger says:

"*That's ok I'll finish it now.*"

Then consumes the beverage in a single gulp. Now they are getting into my car and they are likely angry at me thinking I am being unreasonable. Should I be expecting a five-star rating and a tip at the end of the ride? Is it likely we will have a great conversation while in route? I think not.

The point is this: If you as a rideshare driver start a conversation with a passenger, or a potential passenger, be prepared for where the conversation may go. In most cases I suggest the best conversation is no conversation at all.

The TNCs expect you to explain why you are refusing to pick a passenger up, however; and this is a very important point for rideshare drivers; you are alone in your car, there isn't a TNC representative in a back office ready to intervene if something troubling happens, whatever happens it's up to you.

The best way to deal with potentially negative situations is to avoid them. I'm not at all interested in matching wits with someone who is behaving poorly, I just want to continue with my day and make money to pay my bills.

Every rideshare driver must choose how to deal with the occasional unreasonable passenger expectation.

My most likely response is to "Cancel/No Charge" and continue with my day, I'm not going to invite a negative situation into my workday and certainly not going to invite a negative situation with a stranger traveling in my car, I'm on the road to make money and everything else is secondary.

If someone's actions outside of my car suggest they may not ride respectfully, I think: *"Thank you but no, I'll pass on this trip, you are not the only passenger needing a ride."*

Again, if you are refusing a trip at the curb, face-to-face with the passenger, the TNCs expect you to explain why. But they have no control over how drivers manage rides or what drivers say to passengers, the TNCs cannot risk treating rideshare drivers like employees.

You do not have to justify your decisions to anyone. I do not negotiate with passengers, and I typically will not explain my actions, I've made my decision, I cancel the business transaction in a professional way, then I drive away.

Some explanations for a canceled trip are simple. When I pull up to an adult with a child too small to ride legally without an appropriate car seat or booster seat, I lock the doors and say:

"Hello, do you have a car seat/booster seat for your child?"

They say: *"No."*

I say: *"I'm sorry I can't take you then, I will cancel the ride and you will not be charged."*

I do not negotiate, I don't not try to be an expert on what kind of car seat or booster seat a child should have when traveling in a car, I do not speak at all until I've made up my mind to say "No."

Adults with children and no car seat is also a statistically rare occurrence. When this has happened to me the responses I've heard have been memorable.

"Oh, I don't use car seats when we ride in taxis."

"Other drivers have taken us."

"It's ok, you're just taking us to Walmart."

After explaining that I've canceled the ride and they would not be charged one adult said:

"You're kidding me?"

Guilt, shaming, and peer pressure are powerful human motivators, don't buy in, make your decision then speak professionally and with authority.

Are You

Kidding Me?!

Resist the urge to say something witty, you are alone, you are making all the decisions, you are out there rideshare driving to make money and everything else is secondary.

To the woman who said: *"You're kidding me"* I could have said:

"Uhhh… no I'm not kidding you, I'm not a comedian, I am an independent rideshare driver."

To the woman who said: *"Other drivers have taken us"* I said:

"Uber drivers are independent contractors; the next driver you call will probably take you."

Obviously, I have no idea if the next driver will transport the child without an appropriate car seat/booster seat but not my problem. I stay professional, say as little as possible, and go on with my day.

I'm not going to tell a potential passenger they are putting us both at risk for a criminal charge, not a traffic ticket, a criminal charge: "Reckless endangerment of a child."

As a father of two elementary-aged children how would that look on my permanent record? Pretty sure I would no longer pass the school's background check required for me to attend a holiday party in my kid's classroom.

When passengers expect to squeeze too many passengers I could talk about no insurance coverage and excessive wear on my small Toyota Prius, but I don't, I say:

"I've canceled this ride and you will not be charged. You can call another driver."

I could tell the twenty-something man that an open alcoholic beverage in a moving vehicle is illegal in Colorado. I could say that I didn't want him spilling alcohol in my car.

135

Think about that passenger for a moment, if I had allowed him in my car it would be my responsibility to drive very carefully, or a spill would be my fault? Yeah, I'm thinking: "No."

When you accept any passenger's behavior that happens before you choose "Start Trip" you have communicated without saying anything that you have no issue with what they are doing.

What's most difficult is noticing the open beverage or something else after the passenger is in the car.

After my few months of always locked doors, I typically have my doors unlocked at the pick-up location and it's common for passengers to approach from behind my car, so I do not always get a good look at a new passenger before they are in my backseat.

Depending on the circumstance I am mentally prepared and have a plan, I am ready to "Cancel/No Charge" the ride and ask the passenger(s) to exit the car. It will not be fun to eject someone from my car but once they are out of the car I'll drive away, and the situation will be over.

When I first started driving it was tempting to tell the food-eating passengers: "*No, you may not eat in my car*" then take them where they wanted to go.

It was tempting only because I was afraid. Afraid I wouldn't get another Trip Request soon and I wouldn't make "enough" money.

I usually do allow people to eat in my car, when they ask, and if what they propose to eat or drink does not seem likely to make a mess. I usually say: "*Yes, please be neat, and thank you for asking first.*"

In my first few months rideshare driving I took two college-aged women to McDonald's and after they had their food they immediately started eating without asking. After the drop-off I saw there was lettuce and crumbs all over the backseat.

I wasn't mentally prepared for them and I did not have a plan. I assumed they would behave the way I would behave in a stranger's personal car, I was wrong.

I didn't even know I could have taken photos of the mess, opened a support ticket with the TNC and possibly gotten a little extra money.

Rideshare passengers are contractually obligated to pay for messes they make in a rideshare driver's car, typically up to $250.

If I had taken a photo of the lettuce and crumbs on the backseat, then opened a support ticket, I probably could have gotten about $30 and the passengers would have learned a lesson when they saw the bill.

Once again it is important rideshare drivers always have their minds right and be mentally prepared with a plan!

Because I understand that my earnings will always average out over time; my working mindset is always:

"*I don't need this fare.*"

When I have my mind right, it is easier to just say "No."

RIDESHARE DRIVERS ARE INDEPENDENT CONTRACTORS – Drivers control "The ride."

An independent contractor can say "No" for any reason other than the legal definition of discrimination.

Discrimination = Federal laws, supplemented by court decisions, prohibit discrimination in such areas as employment, housing, voting rights, education, and access to public facilities. They also proscribe discrimination on the basis of race, age, sex, nationality, disability, or religion.

How you manage your rideshare rides is entirely up to you. You are not an employee of the Transportation Network Company or TNC, you are a private contractor accepting (or not) work offered by the TNC.

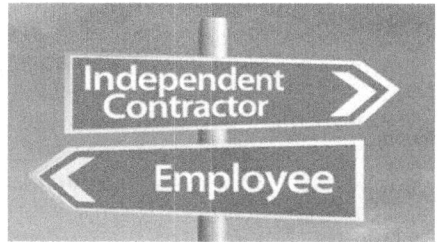

One of the questions determining if a worker is an employee or and independent contractor is:

"***Does the company control or have the right to control what the worker does and how the worker does the job*?**"

The "job" is safely transporting passengers from Point A to Point B.

How you manage the rides is up to you. And as a contractor and not an employee you have the right to choose what work you are willing to do.

MULTIPLE OPPORTUNIITES TO SAY "NO"

There are at least three points where I might say "No" before choosing the TNC "Start Trip" option and transporting passengers.

The first one is easy, you get "pinged" on your phone with a Trip Request and let it go by without accepting. Always your choice and don't worry about your "Acceptance Rate" unless you have a good reason to care.

A "good reason to care" will always be about making money, you may be working an active Promotion or Bonus offer that requires you to accept every Trip Request, or have an "Acceptance Rate over 90%" during the offer.

If you let even one Trip Request go by without accepting you might "lose" the extra income, read Promotion and Bonus offer requirements carefully. "90% Acceptance Rate" might mean you are accepting 9 of 10 Trip Requests, if you only have to give 10 rides to earn the income you can only let one Trip Request go by without accepting.

I'm not telling you to drive 20 minutes or more to a pick-up location, just know the offer details and make an informed decision. Remember to drive safely, it will often make sense to accept every Trip Request and decide if you want to "Cancel/No Charge" when it's safe to consider what you want to do.

Losing a $6 bonus because you didn't want to drive over 20 minutes without a paying passenger is probably not going to affect your average hourly income.

The second opportunity to say: "No" before picking up a passenger is when you are on route to the pick-up location and decide to choose the "Cancel/No Charge" option for any reason. At this point all you know about the passenger is a first name and a pick-up location; you can't violate the legal definition of discriminate against a name or a location.

You are making a business decision to not accept the work... it is always up to you.

Third (and probably the hardest) is at pick-up location with the potential passenger face-to-face and hopefully not in your car yet.

I drove for months keeping my doors locked at the pick-up location and requiring every passenger to verbally confirm the name on the Trip Request before I unlocked the doors.

Keeping doors locked protects driver safety and gives drivers control over who gets into their cars. Saying "No" is easiest before people are in your car.

Most passengers in Denver/Boulder, Colorado expect the Uber/Lyft door to be unlocked and almost always pull on the handle without saying anything while outside the car.

My front windows are always open at least a little bit at the pick-up location, and I will often say: "Hello" when the passenger is approaching my car and close enough to hear me. The most common response when passengers are still outside my car has been: "Hello" then they pull on the door handle.

If my door is locked most passengers will wait a second then pull on the handle again, thinking I forgot to unlock the doors and expect me to unlock the door without talking to them.

During the months that I kept the doors locked, until I confirmed the name on the Trip Request, I would often have to say: *"Hello?"* to call them up to the open front window. Then I would say: *"What is the name on the Trip Request?"* After they responded with the correct name I would unlock the doors.

In my perfect rideshare transportation world every rideshare driver would keep their doors locked until confirming the passenger name.

If almost every driver's doors were locked at the pick-up location passengers would learn to expect locked doors until they spoke to the driver.

If I were female I would probably always keep the doors locked until I was sure I was going to transport the passengers. For the record, I hate that we live in a world where females have to do different things than males to protect their safety.

I am a 6-foot-tall male and I weigh 225 pounds. I am relatively athletic, and I am mentally very comfortable with the idea of confronting another human being if it becomes necessary.

I've driven over 11,000 rideshare trips and I've only had a handful of "bad" experiences and a very small number of passengers I've refused face-to-face.

At least 95% of my rides have been routine. Maybe 4% have been "interesting" for one reason or another. And only 1%, probably less, have been what I would call "bad."

If you keep the doors locked until the name on the Trip Request is confirmed it is likely passengers will pull on your locked door handles. Yes, passengers will probably not "get it" and pull on the handle a second time. You will have to say *"Hello?"* to draw them over to an open window.

After a few months I made the decision locked doors wasn't worth the hassle at pick-up, mostly I was thinking about the first impression passengers made about me as a rideshare driver.

I try not to care about my average star rating as a rideshare driver, but I don't want to get a bunch of 4-star ratings from passengers who do not like that I am doing something most drivers are clearly not doing.

I also didn't like the conversations in my car about why my doors were locked before I had confirmed the name on the Trip Request. I do not want to spend any energy "training" people how to behave and I don't want negative conversation with strangers traveling in my car.

Rideshare driving will always contain an element of luck. You could drive for months and never experience a "bad" passenger or you could get one on your first rideshare trip. The idea is to be prepared with a plan and have a willingness, be mentally prepared, to say "No" sometimes when you are face-to-face with a potential passenger.

When I was locking my doors at the pick-up location, I once had a passenger say:

"Do you really think someone will try to steal a ride in this neighborhood?"

Clearly, she was not thinking about my safety and I guarantee almost all passengers would be surprised to hear me say: *"It is my right to choose."*

I responded to her snotty-sounding comment with: *"I confirm every passenger name before I unlock the doors."*

She got into the car with a friend and nothing more was said about the pick-up.

She might have noticed the sign on my dash saying: "*All trips confirmed before entry*" and "*Parties of two or less please ride in the backseat.*"

While completing this particular ride, I thought about the pickup interaction and I suspected she did not respect my right to have locked doors, but then I asked myself questions:

> "*How many rules do I want to enforce during an 8-hour rideshare driving day?*"

> "*How would I decide when to have the doors locked and when to have them unlocked at the pick-up location?*"

> "*If I'm in 'this' kind of neighborhood I will have unlocked doors but in 'that' kind of neighborhood I will lock my doors?*"

I wondered how I would I make those determinations? I was sure I did not want to make that kind of decision, at every passenger pick-up, part of my standard rideshare driving practices.

If I control the rides, the way I conduct myself when safely transporting passengers from Point A to Point B, then I control my work environment, right?

Controlling the work environment means controlling what kinds of conversations I am not going to start or invite people to have with me.

Yes, the pick-up location was a residential, single-family home; it was a very nice, affluent neighborhood; it was a sunny day around noon; no one else was around...

But when I am rideshare driving, I make the rules.

If I want to lock the doors I will.

And I do not have to respond to everything a passenger says, in fact there will be situations where ignoring something a passenger said is the best option. I could have ignored the woman's snide-sounding comment and simply continued with the name confirmation and unlocking of the doors.

Official Rules

Saying nothing that does not need to be said can be hard, but it is a worthy habit to practice.

Remember that the gig is:

"*Safely (and hopefully politely) transporting passengers from Point A to Point B*."

I also thought about my primary goal:

"*My primary goal is to make money and everything else is secondary*."

I spend as little as possible energy explaining myself and my actions, but I have thought about saying something like:

"Having defined processes and procedures helps me enjoy this job and protects my personal safety and the safety of my personal car."

If you are inclined to explain yourself this phrase could be used in a wide variety of situations.

It's not something I would say because the meta-message (please excuse the psychobabble) could be heard by your passenger as communicating whatever they did or said was in some way "wrong" and inviting a negative interaction with a passenger is something I never want to do.

ENDING A TRIP EARLY – *"YOU'RE OUTTA HERE!"*

In an extreme situation you might choose to end the trip early and drop off a passenger at a safe location before you reach the defined drop-off location.

This is a last resort action.

The best option is almost always completing the trip then immediately calling the TNC support phone number or opening a support ticket describing what happened.

I would only take the: "You're outta here" option in an extreme situation and in over 11,000 completed trips I've taken this option only a couple of times during an active trip.

YOU'RE OUTTA HERE!!!

Once when I took the "You're outta here" option someone vomited in my car. I took the next highway exit and drove to the entrance of a motel near the highway. The motel happened to be conveniently located right off the highway.

At the front door of the motel I asked the passengers to exit my car.

I hope I will always have my mind right when I am rideshare driving.

I do not plan to ever evict a passenger because I took personally something they said or something they did, in other words I never want to take the "You're outta here" action for an emotional reason.

It helps me to remember that a given passenger would have misbehaved in anyone's rideshare car, I just got "lucky" and got them in my car.

Very important: A "safe" location is never asking someone to exit your car on the side of a highway unless you feel physically threatened.

If you feel physically threatened and do eject someone from your car in a potentially unsafe location I suggest calling 911 as soon as you are a safe distance from the ejected passenger.

Remember "First do no harm" means covering yourself for potential liability, if the person you ejected on the highway shoulder is hurt you do not want to be found liable in some obscure way.

If you do call 911 you can say: "*I don't want to press charges I just want to make certain that person is safe."*

Also important, make your decision but do not verbally communicate your intent to eject the passenger(s) from your car until you are at the safe location to eject the passenger.

Have the passengers exit your car at the first parking lot, side street, etc. someplace where a pedestrian would be safe, or at least safe enough. Ideally a well-lit and open retail establishment where the passengers could choose to go inside.

In over 11,000 trips I have thought about ejecting passengers only a few times.

In most cases instead of acting on my emotional response, I've looked at the navigation map and thought:

"*In 5 minutes you will be out of my car and out of my life."*

If you rate a passenger three stars or less the TNC software will automatically make sure you are never matched with that passenger again.

There was another time I ejected someone from my car before the drop-off location; however, we had only traveled about a hundred feet.

The passenger was very drunk and had not entered a drop-off location when requesting the trip. When I asked where he wanted to go, his response, slurring his words badly, was to ask me repeatedly why I didn't know where he wanted to go. I calmly explained he had not put his drop-off location in the application. He kept repeating the same things, wanting to know why I didn't know where he was going when every other driver he had every had knew where he was going... a circular conversation, no thank you.

I pulled up to the curb less than a block from where I had picked him up and asked him to exit the car. He tried to negotiate staying in my car and still getting a ride, but I am very clear in my mind that when I decide to say "No" it will never become a "Yes" so there was nothing further to talk about, I told him:

"There is nothing to discuss, please exit the car."

He continued to negotiate, I repeated:

"There is nothing to discuss, please get out of the car."

I had asked him to exit the car twice, then I entered 911 on my phone's dialing interface and said:

"The next thing I am going to do is call 911 and get the police involved, is that what you want?"

He got out and I drove away.

I want to close this section repeating again, the kind of negative interactions detailed in this section of the book, are extremely rare.

It's not my goal to convince anyone to be a rideshare driver but I don't want you to be scared about the potential for bad situations either.

I spent at least six months often worried that my next passenger would be "one of those" and I was not enjoying being a rideshare driver during that time.

Once I got my mind right knowing I have a plan and am mentally prepared if something goes "wrong" I relaxed and most of the time enjoy rideshare driving as a great way to earn income.

DRIVER'S PERSONAL SAFETY

"Expect the best, plan for the worst, and prepare to be surprised."
~Denis Waitley

Before I made the decision to be a rideshare driver, the most important question on my mind was: *"What about my personal safety?"*

Looking for answers I searched the internet and found news stories and YouTube videos about rideshare drivers with misbehaving passengers.

> *Please watch this YouTube video. Apologies to the driver for using him as an example of what **not** to do. I suspect after this experience, the driver in*

the video changed something, possibly just stopped rideshare driving. Hostile Uber Driver: *https://tinyurl.com/y7z77yhu*

If only he had a simple action plan to get passengers out of his car.

This section of the book will detail a simple process. A simple process I developed over time and perfected with occasional use. This is what I do if things go "south" during one of my rides.

First the basic question of driver safety. Before I made the decision to be a rideshare driver I decided to trust the fact that the person who requested the trip has a credit card registered with the TNC.

The TNCs want to get paid for the millions of Trip Requests they receive each day, so every transaction is validated before the Trip Request is sent to a driver – the TNC knows the credit card is current or the passenger cannot request a trip.

With every trip I know the passenger's personal information is on record with the TNC, so if needed, the passenger's important details are easily traceable.

Also, the person booking the ride knows they can be traced, and will be accountable for their actions; and to at least some extent, the person who requested the trip will be accountable for the actions of the passengers they bring with them.

In over 9,000 trips I've only felt somewhat unsafe once and I suspect the passengers were just hassling me to see how I would react. I was new to the rideshare gig at the time so probably a little nervous how to react (or not) to misbehaving passengers. If I had the trip to do again, I might have used the step-by-step process detailed below to eject them from my car.

Using my step-by-step process, I could have pulled the car over in a safe location said: *"Please exit the car."* If they asked for an explanation: *"I have canceled this trip. Please exit the car"* and if they persisted, wanting to argue: *"There is nothing further to discuss. Please exit the car."*

I am not going to explain to a misbehaving passenger why I'm asking them to exit the car, if I'm taking this extreme action I believe they know why.

If they really don't know why I'm ejecting them from the car they can complain to the TNC. I'm not concerned about the complaints because if anything goes "south" during an active trip (the driver has chosen the "Start Trip" option) I open a written support ticket with the TNC. I want my story on record with the TNC immediately after the "bad" passenger experience.

I use the TNC live phone support occasionally, but for anything important, I want a written, trackable record detailing what happened.

Before we get to the step-by-step process, remember, if you eject passengers from your car it is not logical to argue with them, or even engage in a conversation, stay calm, repeat the same phrases:

- ***"Please exit the car."***
    - o Keep it impersonal, professional, so not "my car" say "the car."
- ***"I have canceled this ride."***
    - o The idea behind leading with the fact that the ride has already been canceled, the ride/trip is over and it's time for me to drive away with an empty car.
- **If true you can say: *"You will not be charged."***
    - o For example, refusing a ride/trip at the pick-up location and using the "Cancel/No Charge" option.
    - o If something "funky" happens, I'm not concerned with getting paid, I'm focused on completing the interaction and driving away with an empty car.
- **"There is nothing to discuss."**
    - o I not engage in arguments. I do not over-explain my actions and in most cases I don't explain them at all. My goal is always driving away with an empty car not engaging in a pointless conversation.

When you are rideshare driving I suggest you only say out loud actions you are really willing to do. Don't be the mom/dad on a road trip telling the kids: *"If you don't stop [behavior] I will pull over and..."*

Try to stay as neutral as possible, the best choice is usually finishing the ride/trip thinking: *"In 5 minutes this passenger will be out of my car."*

If you decide to eject passengers from your car, use the process described below, or define your own process, the point is to have a plan just in case.

Having a plan and being mentally prepared to execute the plan if necessary, made a huge difference for me, I went from being almost constantly worried about future passengers to being relaxed, rideshare driving became more routine and less like a ticking bomb with me nervously waiting for "the bomb" of a "bad" passenger experience to explode.

In a recent example, a group of five, well-dressed, over 40-somethings wanted to overload my car. I didn't have to think about what to do, I locked my doors, canceled the trip choosing the "Cancel/No Charge" option, told the potential passengers they could call another driver, drove away. As I was driving away I thought: "That was easy!"

It was easy and did not ruin a moment of my day in spite of the fact that one man was yelling at me, saying repeatedly: "*What is your name?*" I guess he wanted my name, so he could try to get me fired? I think he was just trying to be intimidating.

Unlikely he would even contact the TNC, because he would have to lie about why I did not pick them up. I didn't bother to open a support ticket because I did not choose the "Start Trip" option.

If I was contacted by the TNC support organization I would have remembered the canceled trip and explained they expected me to break the law by overloading my car with passengers.

You are a private contractor and you are alone with no backup. There is no on-site manager to take over a difficult situation; what happens during your rides is 100% up to you.

You are not an employee and do not have to take any abuse... that's right, you do not have to tolerate any abuse!

The TNCs do not, and really cannot, tell you exactly what to do if things go wrong during a trip. You are a private contractor. The TNCs cannot risk treating you like an employee. What you do, the actions you take, are entirely up to you.

Here is my safety plan in case things go really "south."

1. **I decide I'm done with the passengers.**
   - It's unlikely I have said anything suggesting I was thinking about ejecting them or even frustrated with their behavior.
   - I navigate to a safe location.
   - If a passenger asks what's up I will say: "I need to pull over for a second."

2. **I stop my car in a safe location**, ideally a brightly lit location, maybe in front of an open store or hotel, whatever is available close to the current location.
   - Stopping on the side of a highway is not a safe place for you or your car, and not a safe place to leave a passenger - unless of course if you feel physically threatened.

148

- I don't want to leave anyone "in the middle of nowhere" but I'm not willing to spend much time achieving my goal, which is driving away with an empty car.
- After I've made the mental decision to eject someone from my car I'm not going to look for an ideal spot for more than a minute or two. I may have to settle for dropping the passengers off at any safe location to be a pedestrian.
- The passenger has a smart phone and a TNC application loaded on their phone, they can call another ride, or walk, or whatever. My only concern is my personal safety and potential for future liability.
- The side of a highway is not a safe place to be a pedestrian. If someone were injured, they can claim the rideshare driver had some liability because the driver ejected them from the car at an unsafe location. It doesn't matter if you are found not liable, it costs money to be sued.

3. **I turn on my phone's video camera using the forward-facing camera.** My goal is to record my actions, what I do and what I say.
   "*I am recording and asking you to please exit the car.*"
   - I make sure the passenger can see the screen of my phone.
   - You are expecting the passengers to exit the car. If they want to argue the only thing I will say is: "There is nothing to discuss."
   - Seeing themselves on my phone's display gets the passenger's attention. If the camera recording is ever needed you will be defending your actions, you may want to look at the camera too.

4. **If necessary I will calmly repeat:**
   "*Please exit the car.*"
   - Think business transaction, not personal. You are executing a business policy. I suggest saying "the car" not "my car" because it sounds more professional.

5. **I am not making a request**; the passenger needs to exit my car and does not have a choice in the matter. Repeating for the final time:

"*Please exit the car.*"
And as needed:
"*There is nothing to discuss.*"

- Ejecting someone from your car is an extreme action.
- It's likely the passenger will "play dumb" as to why they are being ejected from the car. Passengers have asked me to explain my actions or tried to engage me in whatever line of thinking they think applies. My response is always the same: "*There is nothing to discuss*" and "*Please exit the car.*"
- I don't have to explain myself and I'm not going to: "*There is nothing to discuss.*"
- I don't want to say: "*Please exit the car*" too often or it will sound like I don't have a next step.

6. **At this point I've said: "Please exit the car" three, maybe four times.** I take a moment to decide if I think the passenger will be giving up soon.
   - I'm hoping the passenger will give up and exit, I might repeat "*Please exit the car*" but I will continue to be calm and professional.
   - Depending on the situation and my assessment of the passenger I might only say "*Please exit the car*" once or twice moving more quickly to the next step.

7. **If I think extreme action will be required to clear passengers from my car I say:**
   "*The next thing I am going to do is call 911 and get the police involved - is that what you want?*"
   - I won't play this card lightly. I don't want to escalate a situation if a little patience will get the passenger out of the car.
   - I don't want to burden the emergency response system in my city by calling 911 unless I think it's the only way to get the passenger out of the car.
   - If I get to Step 7, it is the passenger's last chance to exit the car, they have only a few seconds to start getting out before I go immediately to step eight.
   - Remember there is no way to know what a human being might do next... err to the side of caution.

8. **I call 911 on the speakerphone.**
    - I don't worry about responding to the 911 operator they will hear what is going on and understand what I am doing.
    - When I hear: ***"911 what is your emergency?"*** The 911 operator will hear me say: ***"The 911 operator is on the line please exit the car now."***

9. **After the passenger exits the car** I will talk to the 911 operator and explain that I am an Uber driver and had passengers making me feel unsafe.
    - I keep it simple, the 911 operator just needs to know if police or emergency responders need to be sent.
    - Once I had a whole conversation with the 911 operator and the passenger just sat quietly in the back seat even after hearing that the police were on their way.

10. **In the very unlikely case that the passengers will still not exit the car** and I know the 911 operator is on the line listening, I repeat as calmly as possible: ***"Please exit the car."***
    I hope I won't have to say: ***"911 Operator I need police dispatched to my location."***
    - The 911 call record will defend your appropriate actions.
    - 911 does not make distinctions what actions are "appropriate," if you feel unsafe that is enough to warrant a call to 911.
    - Even a passenger who is not being physically threatening is a risk, you are not safe if a passenger is refusing to exit your car.

I have used this plan but have only reached Step #8 a couple of times. In over 11,000 rideshare driving trips I've only called 911 twice, usually seeing that I am ready to dial 911 is enough.

If I someday find myself at Step 10 or beyond I will focus on my safety. The car doesn't matter, my stuff doesn't matter, all that really matters is my safety.

I hope you will not get too caught up worrying about things that may never happen. If thinking about having a plan, and thinking about being mentally prepared to ask someone to exit your car, causes excessive anxiety, maybe rideshare driving is not right for you?

In one of my college psychology courses I heard the term: "Evil World Syndrome" used to describe how mainstream media reporting can cause us to believe the world is generally unsafe, "evil."

Since mainstream media typically spends the most energy on reporting the worst of the worst stories, it's easy to believe bad stuff is happening everywhere when the reality is most rideshare drivers will never be a situation to reach Step #8 and actually call 911.

When misbehaving passengers hear: "*The next thing I'm going to do is call 911 and get the police involved, is that what you want?*" (Step 7) Most passengers will exit your car immediately.

Misbehaving passengers typically have reasons to not want to interact with the police, for example if they have a more than a couple of alcoholic beverages.

It is also unlikely you will ever be in a situation where it would be safer for you to abandon your car; however, be mentally and physically prepared to see this as an option. As example, my Toyota Prius has keyless ignition and the keys are always in my pocket not in the ignition slot.

If I'm using this step-by-step process, I know I will be holding my phone and it will be actively recording what is happening, (Step 3) and if I exit the car (Step 10) my phone and my keys are with me. I'm as safe as I can be, I have my phone, passengers cannot drive away with my car, and I am on the line with a 911 operator.

Again, it is very unlikely you will need Steps 8, 9, and 10; unlikely you will ever need to use the threat of police (Step 7.)

I strongly suggest new rideshare drivers mentally prepare themselves in advance for a worse-case scenario. Be mentally prepared, have a plan of action, have peace of mind.

In over 11,000 trips I would only describe three or four additional trips as seriously "bad." I'm defining "bad" as feeling extremely relieved when the passenger exited my car.

I'm not talking about being a little annoyed. I find some passengers mildly annoying and am relieved when they exit my car. A few annoying passengers are part of the gig and what human beings find annoying is personal, what bugs me might not bug you.

The two times I actually called 911 (Step 9) my personal safety was probably not an issue, but the passengers were not exiting the car and until they did exit anything could have happened next.

The woman who would not exit the car was part of a group of seven people trying to get into my car without asking if it was ok.

My Prius legally transports only four passengers and one driver, having seven people trying to get into the car without asking felt like an April Fool's prank, but it was not April 1st.

The passengers were talking loudly to each other giving me no opportunity to speak. Three people were in the backseat soon after I pulled up to the curb, the rest were crowded up to the open doors, clearly all seven were planning to squeeze in. No one had said anything to me or even given me the opportunity to speak.

I made my decision, "No", since they were being so loud I couldn't talk without yelling so I calmly selected the "Cancel/No Charge" option then I raised my voice a little to say: "Excuse me?"

They stopped talking.

Then I said: "*I have canceled this ride. You will not be charged, please exit the car.*"

Most of the passengers exited immediately but one woman in the backseat did not, she wasn't going without a fight, but I didn't give her one.

She wanted to argue with me, said that I should take four passengers letting the other passengers call another driver. And she wasn't asking me if I would transport four passengers, she was telling me, as if I were her employee or at least an employee of the TNC without the option of saying "No."

The specifics of what she was saying were irrelevant to me. Once I decide the answer is "No" there really isn't anything to discuss. She needed to get out of the car.

Soon after the 911 operator was on speakerphone someone from the group of seven reached into the car and pulled her out. I drove away and explained the situation to the 911 operator. The 911 operators key questions were: "Do you need the police?" and "Do you want to press charges?"

In my life, in the actions I take, I don't say "No" lightly; a habit honed during years working professionally with kids and teenagers.

People need clear boundaries... and when I am rideshare driving I need clear boundaries too... and a mental willingness to enforce my boundaries.

For rideshare drivers the boundaries should be simple and make sense to you.

I have very few rules and possibly the most important one is - I'm not going to feel unsafe or completely disrespected; and I know what to do if "bad" things happen. I have a plan and I am mentally prepared to execute my plan.

When passengers are troublesome it may help to think like a parent.

WHY DO PEOPLE DISCUSS USELESS THINGS AND THEN COMPLAIN WHEN NOTHING GETS DONE?

My children know that once I have said "No" I will never change my answer to "Yes" because I never have.

If my kids thought they could change my "No" to a "Yes" I would be constantly trying to justify my reasons for saying "No" because they would always remember the time where they were able to convince me.

My kids also know I am unlikely to explain why I said "No" and unlikely to engage in much, if any, discussion about my decision.

Do not engage in specifics as a rideshare driver either:

"There is nothing to discuss."

Also true, like a savvy parent I am careful to never say I am going to do something unless I am willing to take that action.

I will never say: *"If you don't stop [whatever] I will [whatever]."*

I won't say anything until I have already decided the answer to the situation is some version of "No". Then the only thing that needs to happen is me driving away in an empty car.

If I'm saying "No" I never want to sound harsh, I always approach my rideshare driving business as a professional, and I always conduct myself in a professional manner, a manner I believe is beyond reproach.

Every situation will be different, stay as neutral as possible to whatever is happening and keep your actions simple.

If you are feeling really "bugged" the best plan is probably completing the trip and letting the passengers exit your car without being ejected.

After your car is empty and you've driven away rate passengers three stars or less. Three stars of less insures you will never be matched with that passenger again.

I'm the boss and for all practical purposes I report only to me. I appreciate this freedom and I do not abuse it, I want to feel good about what I do, feel good about the actions I take as a rideshare driver.

In the past two years of rideshare driving I've learned that worrying about what might happen next is an unpleasant way to spend my rideshare driving shifts.

I've also learned it is usually difficult to remember details of yesterday's great conversations, but I remember the "bad" experiences with passenger for much longer.

When I am rideshare driving my goal is to be neutral in my thinking, I want to enjoy my rideshare driving gig.

The bad experiences still stay with me, but my plan of action helps me spend less energy worrying about the next passenger.

When I'm worrying about a future passenger's behavior it is not fair to me or my current passengers. I don't want to be grumpy with a passenger because I'm worrying about a future passenger.

Simply put, I want to have "My Mind Right."

YOUR ACHILLES HEEL?

One or more common, recurring, rideshare driving circumstances may almost always make you feel "on edge" or "push your buttons." It helps to identify them, I call mine my "Achilles Heels."

I wrote this section hoping that sharing some of my weaknesses will help you identify and make peace with any "weaknesses" you may have as a rideshare driver.

Defining my weaknesses also gives me the opportunity to share a few additional thoughts I believe will be helpful to every rideshare driver.

In my first month or so of rideshare driving I realized that it was a "job" where it would be possible to be upset about something almost every moment I was out on the road... that's not how I want to spend my work days.

I want to spend most of my waking hours feeling good, so I made the choice to make peace with rideshare driving.

In work settings I've always said: "If we're not having some fun, we're not doing it right!"

After two years on the road and over 9,000 trips, the things that bothered me at first don't bother me anymore – or at least not as much, or not as often.

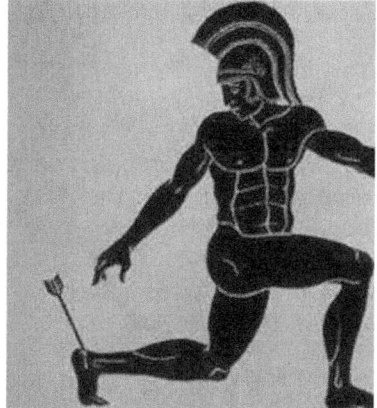

When I first started driving it seemed like I had a "bad" story to tell almost every day I drove. Now it's rare I feel "bugged" during a shift and when a passenger asks: "What is your worst experience as a rideshare driver?" I am telling stories that happened months or over a year previous.

There are three recurring circumstances that almost always put me on edge.

Again, I'm sharing details of what bothers me hoping it will help you identify, live with, and eventually conquer things that will almost always bother you during your rideshare driving days:

1. **Pedestrians – People who live in Colorado love to point out: "In Colorado the pedestrian always has the right-of-way." And before I started rideshare driving I thought this sounded pretty**

cool. I have a very different take on it now, I've seen the way pedestrians can behave, at least in Colorado.

Pedestrians will cross streets anywhere and often without obviously looking both ways. They seem to assume oncoming traffic will slow down or stop for them and there is nothing for them to worry about.

Personally, when I am a pedestrian, I'm concerned that a physical encounter with a car or truck will ruin my day, week, month, year, lifetime...

I don't understand pedestrian behavior at all. When crossing a street, I've taught my kids to always: *"Cross like you have someplace to be, move quickly."*

I've taught them it doesn't matter if the street is busy or quiet or if a parking lot is busy or quiet: *"If there is the possibility of a car or truck driving where you are walking then move quickly."*

This is how my father taught me to behave around cars and trucks. With my kids I constantly harp on being safe around cars. I want them to build habits that will keep them safe for life, even when they are distracted.

Some pedestrians even seem to expect oncoming cars to anticipate how quickly they are walking down a sidewalk toward an intersection, they will not break stride as the walk right into the street in front of my car.

These pedestrians seem oblivious to the fact that drivers are watching the road not the sidewalks; I can't see as well in the dark; I can't see as well if the sun is in my eyes; I might be distracted by something in the car; etc.

The flip side of walking into the street without pausing, pedestrians will linger at a street corner and sometimes even stand physically in the street, past the curb. Their position or body language communicates they might be about to cross the street.

To be safe, I must slow down just in case, while thinking: *"Are you going to cross or what?"*

At crosswalks pedestrians will often ignore the don't walk light, the "Big Red Hand" sign.

If most pedestrians respected the "Big Red Hand" I would be able to make a right or left-hand turn without as much stress. Since so many pedestrians ignore the "Big Red Hand" every time there is a pedestrian standing on the curb I have to slow down where my car is almost stopped, or even have to stop just in case.

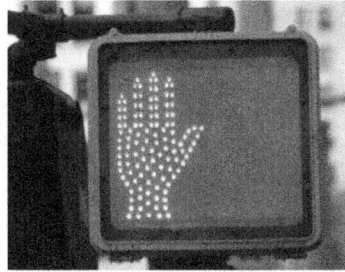

My dad taught me never to cross in front of a car unless you have made eye contact with the driver, unless you've made eye contact you don't know if the driver has seen you.

It just makes sense, am I right?

Before rideshare driving I don't think I paid much attention to pedestrian behavior, possibly because I was rarely in a situation where it mattered.

As a rideshare driver I am in high pedestrian traffic areas almost every time I drive.

Crowds of Pedestrians

When a big event ends, pedestrians will sometimes cross an intersection or street in a continuous stream. This can also happen in a city's downtown area, particularly in zones dense with bars and restaurants.

Large groups of pedestrians often behave as if there is safety in numbers and cross intersections in a continuous stream, making it impossible for cars to progress.

In Denver we have busy areas, "Hot Spots", including LoDo (Lower Downtown) and LoHi (Lower Highlands Neighborhood) and RiNo (River North Art District); three areas a lot of people frequent on nights and weekends making them good places to rideshare drive, and likely places to get blocked or slowed down by pedestrian traffic.

When there is a continuous stream of pedestrian traffic blocking my ability to move my car forward, I'll wait a bit for a chance to advance (I'm hoping for a break in the crowd) Eventually I will inch my car forward forcing the crowd to yield the right-of-way. I don't want to be obnoxious, just a chance to go where I'm going too.

Countless times I've seen other drivers, often other rideshare drivers, showing frustration at pedestrians only to have a pedestrian purposefully stop in front of them blocking their ability to move forward.

In these instances, I've seen countless pedestrians dance around in front of the obviously frustrated driver; people who have been drinking alcohol don't always behave in a rational manner.

Remember: "*If you don't want people getting your goat... don't let them know where you tied it up.*"

Another place I've seen this crowd-mentality, pedestrian behavior, is on Boulder's Pearl Street walking mall.

Boulder, Colorado's historic Pearl Street walking mall has cross streets on every block of the pedestrian-only walking mall. The cross streets do not have traffic lights, just a stop sign for the cars. During a busy Saturday afternoon or one of the many street festivals, streams of pedestrians cross seemingly non-stop. Eventually I inch forward as politely as possible.

I will wait a bit, then inch my car forward; I don't want to be obnoxious I'm just out here making money and I get to take a turn too.

The only time this "inching forward" technique seems to bring out the worst in the crowd's behavior is when they have been drinking alcohol to excess.

I've been cursed at by pedestrians; my car has been slapped (loud noise, no damage) and since there was a crowd of people passing I have no idea who did it; and I've been surrounded by pedestrians, a very disconcerting feeling.

I've had people hold up their hand or finger in admonishing ways... obscene gestures and sometimes in a parental, disapproval way, wagging their index finger. It can be extremely difficult not to let my frustration show on my face.

During my first few months as a rideshare driver I knew it was time for a break or to just go home when I heard myself yelling (without passengers in my car):

"Big Red Hand people, what do you think the Big Red Hand means?"

Typically, I try not to care about passenger's behavior; I'm focused on making money, but pedestrian behavior is one of my personal "Achilles Heels."

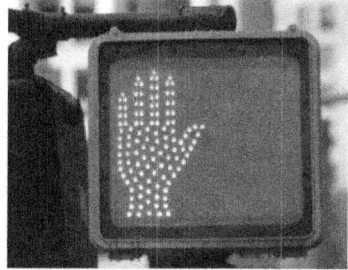

Sometimes I'm not neutral in my thinking, and I don't behave in a positive way, I "lose it" a bit. When this happens, I try to go easy on myself.

I've found it can be very therapeutic to let out my frustrations by yelling something in my empty car:

"What's wrong with you, you stupid @#$%!!!"

If I had a stand-up comedy routine, I might ask the audience a question:

"I get it, in Colorado the pedestrian always has the right of way, but what does that mean exactly? Could someone tell me where a pedestrian does not always have the right of way? In which states is it acceptable to run over a pedestrian with my car?"

When I notice feeling increased stress, I take a breath, take the TNC Apps offline, and take a break.

Don't be afraid of turning off the TNC apps for a few minutes, earnings average out over time and since there is no way of knowing when the next Trip Request will be offered, your first priority as a rideshare driver should be taking care of yourself.

Rideshare driver "rookies" are online while relieving themselves in the convenience store bathroom. When I was a "rookie" I did, now I take my bathroom break offline.

My second Achilles Heel is silly but it bugs me...

   2.   **Passengers who ask me "Is it busy tonight?"**

I can tell myself this greeting is just another way of saying: *"How are you today?"* but the question always seems to bug me at least a little.

160

I'm getting better and someday might be able to eliminate this "Achilles Heel" but for a long time the question bugged me, a lot.

Almost everyone, at least occasionally says: *"How are you today"*, I think they are mostly just to be polite not asking for or expecting a detailed response.

Traveling by rideshare is growing rapidly and it is new to a lot of people. Passengers asking me: *"Is it busy today?"* haven't thought about the question as much as I have.

These passengers probably don't know what is the "right" thing to say when they get in a rideshare driver's personal car, they are just being polite.

Sometimes I find myself giving complicated answers to passengers instead of keeping it simple.

"You busy?"

I could say:

"Thank you, yes, I'm having a good day"

or even just:

"Yes, it's busy today."

I would never say: "No" because this would be inviting a potentially negative conversation.

I think this question bugs me, at least in part, because it feels like they are asking about my income, a question most people wouldn't ask anyone.

In a stand-up comedy routine, my response might be:

"No, it's not 'busy tonight' and, frankly speaking, I hope your destination is a round-trip, and I hope your round-trip destination is 50 miles away because I want to earn a big fare then return to this exact spot; busy downtown area and close to my home.

If I earn a big fare I might be able to pay my rent on time; and after I drop

you off I can continue to get lots of Trip Requests rather than being stranded 50 miles away from here.

What's that, oh you say this will be only a short trip and you want me to wait for you outside the 7-11 while you buy a pack of smokes?

Well, my income is primarily from the trip mileage and not the much smaller amount I earn while waiting for you... but sure, no problem, let's go, BIG FUN!

Oh, what's that? You say you'll tip me on the App, oh thank you... you're very kind."

> Side note: if a passenger says: "*I'll tip you on the App.*" Don't hold your breath. I usually do not see a tip from passengers who say "*I'll tip you on the App.*"

When someone asks me: "*Are you busy tonight?*" I feel obligated to respond with something positive.

I might be well-aware I'm not making great money; I might know I only had a bunch of short rides, but what good would it do to tell a passenger that? If my response is anything but positive I'm inviting a negative conversation in my car.

This question bugs me in part because I think no one would ask a businessperson:

"*Are you making as much money as you hoped or are you thinking about cutting your losses, closing this business, and calling it quits?*"

I believe if passengers thought about it at all, they would figure out that: "*Have you been busy tonight...*" is an inappropriate question to ask a rideshare driver.

More for my stand-up routine, when a passenger says: "*Busy tonight?*":

"No!!! And this is my personal car and it wasn't free, and neither is gas or maintenance. My personal car is not going up in value because I'm racking up mileage using it to rideshare drive.

Seriously this isn't rocket science, is it? No, I've not been 'Busy tonight' and I'm worried about paying this month's rent on time.

And how's your day going, do you make 'enough' money at your job? Are you having concerns about paying your rent on time? When you are

working do your customers expect you to answer questions about how much money you are making?"

Seriously, "Are you busy tonight?" has to be, at least subconsciously, a question about earnings, right?

Rideshare drivers are not paid an hourly wage and their earnings are not guaranteed and if they were thinking about it anyone asking the question: "Busy tonight?" is probably well aware of at least the basics of how drivers are paid?

Passengers who regularly ask their drivers: "Busy tonight" have probably gotten all kinds of answers from different drivers.

Maybe hearing different answers to the question is entertaining?

Some rideshare drivers are aggressively trying to sign up new rideshare drivers to earn a new driver referral bonus.

These rideshare drivers might be giving best-case earnings scenarios or even lying outright about how much money they earn as a rideshare driver hoping to sign up passengers to be new drivers, so of course their answer to "Busy tonight" is something like:

"Holy cow, I'm making money hand over fist every night!"

Passengers who have experienced this kind of driver might think every driver is making more money than they really are and maybe even hoping passengers are going to ask: "*Is it busy tonight?*" so they can talk about how much money they are earning.

Ok, ok, I know I should give a simple answer to the question, but for some reason the question: "Busy tonight", feels like the passenger wants me to talk in detail about my earnings and expenses.

I often wonder if they think rideshare drivers are raking in big bucks doing a relatively stress-free job, and that it is easy to be a rideshare driver because that's what some of their Uber/Lyft drivers have told them.

More stand-up material:

"And I also wonder if the passenger asking me: 'Busy tonight...' believes that even when things 'go south' in my car it's no big deal?

If I passenger disrespects me or throws up in my car I haven't really lost anything, right? In fact, I've "earned" a valuable experience and come away with a great story to tell.

A story I can use to entertain who?

My future rideshare passengers?

Hey that's cool, I get to entertain my future passengers, and I get to relive the negative experience over and over all with little chance of getting a tip! Lucky me!

Yes; it's really busy tonight, and I'm making money hand over fist!

Add to that I always have BIG FUN rideshare driving; I always get happy and respectful passengers; my passengers give me lots of big tips; I always earn big fares; and all the time I'm having fun, fun, fun!!!

By the way did you see the recent article about rideshare drivers not telling the truth? Apparently the rideshare company's star rating

systems tend to motivate drivers to lie for fear if they tell the truth they might be 'rewarded' with a low star rating from the passenger?

Drivers don't want to get a lower star rating because they sound grumpy or negative, so drivers are less likely to tell the truth when answering passenger questions.

Oh, but that's not true for me, I always answer passenger questions truthfully so...

Yes, it is VERY BUSY tonight and I'm making BIG MONEY, and I'm having BIG FUN ALL THE TIME!"

"BUSY" IS BAD AND "SLOW" IS GOOD?

The truth is, before the shared ride trips (Uber Pool and Lyft Shared) were rolled out in Denver the only time I have felt really busy, my "busiest" night of work, I drove four straight hours averaging 5 completed trips per hour during CU Boulder's Parent Weekend.

This level of "busy" was only possible because:

1. I was receiving Trip Requests one on top of the next with little or no waiting for my next Trip Request
2. Each new pick-up location was blocks away from the last drop-off location

In order to complete average five trips every hour for four hours in a row, every trip was a Minimum Fare Trip, making my average hourly rate (not counting any tips I might receive) around $17 an hour.

When I'm getting a mix of short, medium, and long trips I average over $20 an hour.

So "*Yes, it's busy*" but feels like I'm working a lot harder for less money.

Ironically, rideshare driving feels "Slow" to me when I've scored a nice long trip earning $20 or more in a single ride.

So now you might be thinking: "Wait a minute, busy is bad and slow is good?" Are you starting to see my dilemma answering the "Busy tonight" question?

In my stand-up routine I might respond to the "Busy tonight?" passenger with:

"So glad you asked, I love answering that question during a trip where I earn less than four dollars.

I don't even mind that is very unlikely you will leave me a tip for this trip, even though you expect me to: 'Wait outside a store for 5 minutes while you buy a pack of smokes, then you get stuck in a long line at the cashier and it takes more than 5 minutes.

Add to my enjoyment of your awesome company is the fact I drove eight minutes to get to your pick-up location and it took you over four minutes to get into my car... but hey, 12 unpaid minutes in return for the pleasure of your company, I'd make that trade anytime!

No offense intended, after all it was very polite of you to acknowledge your tardiness with the obviously sincere: 'Sorry to keep you waiting' apology you delivered after you walked leisurely to my car looking like you were on an extended vacation at a tropical resort.

So yes!!! It is very busy tonight and I'm so glad you asked!"

This very common passenger question: "*Is it busy tonight*" got me thinking a lot about an appropriate answer. I'm talking months of being extremely bugged by and thinking about the question, after all I spend a lot of time alone in my car, also in my car with passengers who want a quiet ride.

Rideshare drivers have a lot of time to think.

This thought process led me to a realization: I don't want to be busy because busy means a bunch of short trips and low average hourly earnings. I want my rideshare driving days to be "slow but steady" which means my car is almost always full of passengers taking longer trips which equates to higher average hourly earnings.

After having the revelation, I even shared my thoughts with a few passengers, then I realized I did not enjoy the conversations, they often felt negative.

Also annoying, the most common phrasing of this question is: "**Is it** busy tonight" not "**Are you** busy tonight."

Ok I know I'm being too literal now (remember lots of time alone, in my car, thinking) but my standup comedian answer to the question: "Is it busy tonight" would be something like:

"I really don't know if 'IT' is busy tonight because I have no connection to the other drivers on the road. How would I know if 'IT' is busy tonight or not, most nights I drive all over town but what I see on the outside of bars and restaurants is hardly an accurate indication of 'IT' is busy tonight?

Oh, I'm sorry, was that my out loud voice... uhhh, now where am I dropping you off?"

In summary, on the "Busy tonight" question; my goal is to continue to work on being positive and neutral about all the events during my rideshare driving days.

When asked the "Busy tonight" question I'm am currently trying: "Yes it is" or just "Yes" hoping that will be enough of an answer and we can talk about something else. After all, if I ask a cashier at the grocery store: "*How are you today*" I'm not expecting a response other than some version of: "*Fine, thank you.*"

I may have spent too much time writing about my second, personal "Achilles Heel" but I also hoped to make other points, rideshare driving can be frustrating for any number of reasons, the idea of an "Achilles Heel" is they are personal "pet peeves" and can cause a great deal of frustration.

Go easy on yourself and focus on your primary goal for rideshare driving: making money.

My number 3 "Achilles Heel" - Cars and trucks following me too closely namely - TAILGATING.

It took me most of a year and a half and almost 100,000 miles rideshare driving to figure out the probable reason tailgating almost always increases my stress level. Could be... when we are driving the primary dangers are supposed to be in front of the car not behind it?

When someone follows too closely, I feel surrounded by danger, I worry the person behind me could: be distracted by their mobile phone; or not notice that I had to slow down for the car in front of me. I am concerned they will run into the rear of my car for any number of reasons. I want to be focused on the road in front of me, not distracted by what is happening behind my car.

I don't care that the accident will be the tailgaters fault. I haven't been in a single accident for decades, and I don't want to break my string of safe driving.

When you are a rideshare driver, any accident is going to take you off the road, at least to process the accident scene, meaning you cannot earn. Even when an accident is not your fault, it is probable you will have related out-of-pocket expenses along with less time on the road to earn.

The primary point of this section on my: "Achilles Heels"; if you choose to be a rideshare driver it is likely you will discover things that seem to almost always "set you off," it is likely you will sometimes feel "bugged" even after you start to feel comfortable doing a "job" that is unlike any other job.

Feeling "bugged" at times is normal and natural, go easy on yourself.

I have mostly achieved my goal of spending rideshare driving days neutral in my thinking and mostly happy with the work. If you choose to be a rideshare driver I suggest you simply notice when you feel "bugged" without reacting, or over-reacting, and go easy on yourself.

HOT TIPS...

RIDESHARE DRIVER SUPPORT DISCLAIMER

I am not a substitute for TNC support organizations, and neither is RideshareBusinessGuide.com.

RideshareBusinessGuide.com was created to provide fact-based answers to common rideshare driving questions.

RideshareBusinessGuide.com information is not designed to replace TNC's online and live training sessions or the support resources working for the TNCs.

In short it is not the intent of RideshareBusinessGuide.com to be a substitute for the TNC's support organizations; their support staff; or the helpful content they produce.

If you choose to rideshare drive I suggest you watch all of the TNC online training sessions and attend a TNC-sponsored driver's event or two.

If there is one in your city visit the TNC support office. These are things a professional of any occupation would do, take your rideshare driving "position" seriously it will benefit you in the long run.

In-depth technical support is provided by the TNC's support organization - by telephone or using the TNC's support ticket system.

PLAY WITH THE APPS!

Ok, with my: *"I am not a substitute for Lyft/Uber/Other TNCs Support"* disclaimers behind us, I strongly suggest every new rideshare driver "play" with the TNC driver applications and any other application you use while rideshare driving.

Fully explore every menu and drop-down option to see what you find, if a feature doesn't make immediate sense try it and see what happens or follow up as needed with Lyft/Uber/Other TNC support and learn how to use the feature, or maybe learn the feature is not useful to you.

As example, I am very picky about my GPS navigation application settings – I do not like the "Keep map North up" feature; I want the map navigation screen to mirror my car's current direction. I also do not like to keep satellite and traffic overlays turned on, I like a clean interface showing just the streets.

I have experimented with the spoken GPS directions including turning them off for weeks of full-time rideshare driving. I have settled on having the spoken navigation directions turned on just loud enough for me to hear them over my in-car music; even if I can't hear exactly what is being said the sound is a useful reminder that I need to pay attention, there may be a turn coming soon.

Another GPS navigation "trick" I use all the time: It is often useful to look at the map and think about what I am **NOT** going to do next.

As example, I may glance at the map and think: *"I'm not going to turn right on the next two streets, my turn is the third one."* Then I focus on counting the streets leading up to the correct turn.

When there are tricky intersections I often think: *"I'm not taking the hard-left turn, the one I want comes immediately after veering to the left sort of diagonally."*

I know I am repeating myself when I say: "Always go easy on yourself!" After over 150,000 miles rideshare driving I still make navigation mistakes from time to time and sometimes big ones like missing my exit on the highway.

When I've made a "big" mistake that adds a couple of miles or more to the passenger's trip I will tell my passenger:

"I will be opening a support ticket requesting an adjustment to this fare so don't be surprised if you see a charge then a credit sometime after the charge."

Every time I have said this the passenger says: *"Don't worry about it."*

I still open the support ticket and request the fare adjustment in part because I believe owning my mistakes and when appropriate requesting customer refunds communicates to the TNC support organization I approach rideshare driving professionally.

It's unlikely my honesty has any measurable effect on my relationship with the TNC. Still, I'd rather be paid fairly and don't want to earn a few extra bucks which don't feel like "honest" earnings to me.

Someday a TNC representative may have reason to look at my driver history, perhaps because a passenger lodged a complaint against me. What I have written in my past support tickets paints a picture of who I am and could be taken into account when the support resource evaluates the customer complaint.

I believe my years of five-star ratings; written customer compliments; and professional written communication with TNC support resources will make it easy to see through an inaccurate complaint from a vindictive customer.

BE A PRO FROM YOUR FIRST TRIP

The first few months I was a rideshare driver I often felt like people were treating me like some kids treat a substitute teacher.

When you are new to the rideshare driving gig, you will seem "green" to some of your passengers and as result some customers may seem like they are trying to "get your goat."

I know it makes no sense to hassle the driver taking you safely to where you want to be... but it happens.

This kind of passenger behavior rarely happens to me anymore. When a passenger seems likely to misbehave I respond professionally or more often do not respond at all.

I've found no response at all is a powerful tool, it's common the misbehaving passenger settles down probably because I'm not reacting.

When a passenger is being overly distracting while I am thinking about navigation I might say: "*Hold that thought for a moment*" or use some other conversation break like: "*We should be there in about 6 minutes.*"

Anything to communicate I am in charge without directly confronting the passenger. My behavior communicates I am focused on giving safe rides, not providing entertainment.

If a passenger is annoying you for any reason I strongly suggest keeping a "poker face."

Remember this sound advice:

If you don't want people getting your goat don't tell them where you tied it up.

Here are some additional ideas to help your passengers feel like you have been driving for months even though you are new to the rideshare driving gig.

I'm not suggesting new rideshare drivers try to fool their passengers or in any way be dishonest, in fact if it works for you say something like: "*I'm pretty new at this...*"

170

Being honest that you are new to the rideshare driving gig may help you through an uncomfortable situation.

I try to leave my ego at home, I'm not perfect and not trying to be, I try to stay focused on my goal to earn money rideshare driving.

- **You'll like this one: If you want to assert yourself as a confident rideshare driver put out a tip "jar."**

  My tip jar is a ski cap, really a beanie. The hat is attached to my car's dashboard by Velcro strips and is located on the passenger side (My daughter's idea – she is into theater and drama so suggested I "throw out my hat" like a street performer.)

  And my tip hat always has a few dollar bills in it and at least one five-dollar bill in the mix.

  It's possible that the "seed" money looking messy, crumpled up instead of neatly laid out increases the likelihood of a cash tip.

  - One thing is certain, "Tipping on the App" requires the customer to do something after the ride is over and they have at least 24 hours to leave you a tip.

  - The notice passengers receive on their phone from the TNC application and in an email says something like: "We charged your credit card $Xx.xx here is your opportunity to give your driver a star rating and add a tip."

  - Customers do not have to respond to these application pop-up windows or emails, they don't have to respond ever, the TNC will happily charge them for the trip anyway.

  - Don't take it personally if a customer doesn't leave you a tip; they may have forgotten how much "fun" they had during their trip and remember, most passengers do not tip rideshare drivers. It is not personal, it is the passenger's habit to not tip rideshare drivers.

  It took me at least six months of driving before I had the guts to put out a tip jar because of the sensitive nature of "requesting" tips by talking about tips or even passively saying "I accept tips" by displaying a tip jar.

I believe my tip hat communicates without saying a word that I am a service professional delivering a service and communicates: "Yes, I accept tips."

Lyft and Uber have in-app tipping options, but I still have my tip hat displayed on my dashboard.

Funny story: I put out my tip hat the day after I had a Passenger getting off work from his relatively new job as a liquor store cashier. He said when he first started he was surprised to see a tip jar on the counter but thought "why not" so left it out. Over a few weeks he noticed that if the jar started empty it was far less likely for people to leave a tip but if he "seeded" the jar he made about $10 each shift from tips... at a liquor store.

I think my tip hat also communicates: "Some people do tip rideshare drivers" without requiring me to find ways to subtly mention tipping.

From attending rideshare driving events and talking to other rideshare drivers I know some drivers are aggressively talking about tipping rideshare drivers with most of their passengers. I don't care if this technique would earn me extra money, this is just not my style.

I've seen passengers dig into their pockets or wallets to find a couple of bucks when I know they've noticed my tip hat.

Most important to me, I think my tip hat communicates I am not new to the rideshare driving gig. I didn't start rideshare driving yesterday and I'm hopeful potentially troublesome passengers behave better because I don't seem to be "green" or new to the ridesharing gig.

- When I have passengers in my car, I don't answer my phone; I don't read or respond to text messages; and I don't worry about my next trip.
    - o I saw a news article saying a rideshare driver was filmed by his passenger because he was reviewing

profiles in a dating application and even sending text messages to potential dates while he was driving!

- o Don't be "that guy" be safe, crashing your car violates the "first do no harm" suggestion and if you get pulled over by the police you will make less money even if the officer does not give you a ticket.

- If I get a new Trip Request I will accept it and think about the new trip after the current passenger's drop-off. When I have passengers in my car I want to be 100% present for the passengers and the safety of our ride.

    - o It may not seem to make sense that I will not answer my phone when I have passengers in the car even when it is clear the call is from my next passenger.

    - o In my experience, the conversation the next passenger wants to have can be very distracting, I will call them back after the current passenger's drop-off and when I my car is not moving, probably while pulled over out of traffic.

If the current ride is shared, like Uber Pool and Lyft Shared, and I have passengers in the car I might answer the phone on speaker and the conversation will be short and limited to finding the calling passenger.

If the next passenger seems to want a longer conversation I will say: "*I'm driving now and can't talk, I will call you back.*" This usually helps them get to the point of their call.

Sometimes it's kind of funny what people want to say to their driver while on the phone, it's like they have no concept that you are trying to drive safely and follow navigation directions to their pick-up location?

I'm not a super hero able to leap a building in a single bound while navigating a car safely in traffic and talking to someone on the phone.

- o If you want your caller ID to show "Uber" or "Lyft" save every phone number the TNCs uses in your phone's address book.

- o In my phone's address book, I have "Uber 01", "Uber 02", all the way up to "Uber 31" as well as "Uber Notifications" and "Lyft Notifications."
- o The TNCs use blocks of phone numbers to connect passengers with drivers, a practice that insures your personal phone number is never shared with a passenger.

- **Dress like a professional.**
  This doesn't mean wearing a black suit and tie like a limo driver but if you are dressed very casually some people might not treat you like a professional.

  Shorts and a Hawaiian shirt might make sense for a rideshare driver in Honolulu but in Denver this outfit communicates something different.

  - o I don't want passengers thinking the rideshare driving "job" is more about me working in a casual environment and having "BIG FUN" and having "great conversations" with "interesting" people and as an added benefit I am making a little "extra" money.

  - o I seriously doubt the main reason you decided to be a rideshare driver was because it sounded like fun. I believe you wanted to make money, or you would not be a rideshare driver. After you have a few dozen or a few hundred trips under your belt you will realize rideshare driving is a "job" not just a "BIG FUN" way to spend your "extra" time and meet new, "interesting" people.

- **Don't worry if you don't navigate exactly "the right way" when the trip begins.**

  When I was a new driver I often worried about which way to go at the start of a new trip, I never do anymore. I guess I thought a good driver would always take the most-efficient route from the first moment of the trip.

  Certainly, I try to anticipate the best way to travel when a trip starts, but with all Uber passengers I don't know the drop-off location until:
  - o Passengers are in my car
  - o I've confirmed the name on the Trip Request
  - o Chosen the "Start Trip" option.

Since with Uber rides I only see the drop-off location after I choose "Start trip" I usually don't worry about which way I'm going to drive when we pull away from the pick-up location. I just start driving and watch the navigation map screen to confirm I'm headed in a logical direction toward the drop-off location.

Going around the block instead of making a U-turn is not going to make a difference worth worrying about. If it really doesn't make sense to go forward your passenger will probably tell you.

- Google Maps has an option to display the entire route on one screen, using this option to get a quick look at the whole trip can be very helpful.

A quick look after you have confirmed the drop-off location can be very useful and will sometimes tell you it makes sense to start the trip with a U-turn.

  - Again, play with the applications, one reason I'm not trying to provide detailed directions how to use smart phone applications is free applications like Google Maps will roll out updates and changes with little notice, it's free software, it's up to us to figure out how to use it after each new update.

  - The layout of the TNC applications will also change from time to time sometimes without notice. Uber and Lyft driver applications are designed so the software development team can make changes without forcing drivers to download an update, keep your eyes out for subtle changes.

It is very common for me to make a U-turn before passengers get into my car. If it's obvious the best way to start traveling anywhere is turning around (common in residential neighborhoods) and I haven't seen the passenger yet, I turn around before the pick-up.

You may want to ask passengers for suggestions, I try not to let my ego control me, I don't know every twist and turn of every neighborhood in the greater Denver/Boulder location and I do not have a problem with this simple reality.

o   It can be helpful to ask your passenger: *"What's the best way out of your neighborhood?"*

o   If you ask this question some passengers are going to assume you need turn-by-turn directions for the entire trip.

When this happens, I might say: *"Looks like Google Maps has us on the route now, thank you."*

With Lyft passengers I can choose to see the drop-off location after I arrive at the pick-up location and after I select "Confirm Arrival."

• I figured this out once while playing with the Lyft driver application.

• If the Lyft passengers are not waiting at the curb to get immediately into my car, I can look at the drop-off location and mentally prepare my navigation plan.

It was often challenging as a new driver to have no idea where we were going until passengers were in the car watching me, but over time I've grown comfortable with the reality.

When I was a new driver it was tempting to choose the "Start Trip" option before passengers were in the car but now I am committed to never choose "Start Trip" option until I am certain I have the right passengers and I am willing to transport them.

o   With Lyft trips I could look at the drop-off location in advance but usually I do not, I'm not going to refuse a ride because of where we are going, unless of course if the destination is hours away then we'll talk about it.

o   I like to keep my rideshare driving processes simple and repetitive, I don't know where Uber passengers are going so don't care much where Lyft passengers are going, different TNCs but my standard practices are the same.

o   With Lyft trips I usually just wait for the passenger without looking at the drop-off location. In my mind I know when we take off I probably will go "that way" until the GPS application directions kick in.

- **I am knowingly repeating myself because I think this is a very important point:** I strongly advise not peeking at the Uber drop-off Location by selecting "Start trip" before you know you are willing to accept the passenger(s) and the trip they want to take.

  o If you peek you will eventually get "caught" for example with five passengers wanting to get into your four-passenger car and when you try to cancel the trip the TNC application says something like: "You have not traveled far enough to cancel the trip."

  o No worries, you will have to contact the TNC support organization to sort out what happened and make sure you are paid correctly and the passengers are charged appropriately.

You probably don't want to show Uber support a "pattern" by always choosing "Start Trip" as soon as you arrive at the pick-up location (so you can see the drop-off location in advance.)

If there are issues for any reason you might be asked to explain why you are always choosing "Start Trip" before passengers are in your car. To Uber's support representatives it may look like you are screening rides and possibly refusing some rides based on the destination.

Remember if you never chose "Start Trip" the passenger cannot give you a star rating and will have to work more than a little to file a complaint about your behavior with the TNC.

  o The Ice Cream Cone men and women in our world will not be getting rides from me nor will they be able to give me a star rating or be able to easily complain that I refused to transport them and probably did not explain why: *"The driver just said that he canceled the ride and that I would not be charged."*

  o If I refuse to pick someone up because they are holding a melting ice cream cone; or carrying an open (no lid) plastic cup containing an unknown beverage; or because six people were trying to squeeze into my four-passenger car... I think they will be able to figure out why without an explanation from me.

o   I've learned by experience these conversations do not go well, people who think they can treat you and your car like a garbage can are prone to arguing, no thank you, I'll pass on the argument.

You can try to get Uber or Lyft support to pay a cancelation fee because the passengers were trying to overload your car or for some other reason doing something before they got into the car that caused you to refuse to transport them, but it is probably a waste of your time and effort.

o   TNC support organizations are unlikely to make exceptions, you are eligible for a cancelation fee only when the passengers have exceeded the time limit for getting into your car, a "no show."

If passengers do file a complaint, I don't worry about it because independent contractor rideshare drivers have the right to refuse passengers except for reasons included in the legal description of discrimination.

- If the new Uber/Lyft passenger just settled into my car is watching me, they see me "Start Trip" on the TNC driver application only after I have confirmed the name on the Trip Request.

If the new passenger is paying attention to the way I ask to confirm their drop-off location I think it's obvious I did not see the drop-off location until that moment.

If I say: "Drivers do not know where you are going until you are in their car," It is very common for passengers to say:

> *"You don't know where passengers are going until they get in the car? You know I entered my drop-off destination in the App when I requested the trip?"*

It's interesting some passengers express that the reality of not knowing where people are going before picking them up would be enough for them to not want to be rideshare driver.

I stopped worrying about not knowing where passengers were going in advance after about a month of driving; 99.999% of the time I'm willing to go where the passengers are going and every trip is an adventure. No sense being "bugged" by things that are outside of my control.

- If it makes more sense to start with a U-turn; or right turn instead of left out of the neighborhood or apartment complex your passengers will often tell you.

  If they do say: "Thank you" and follow the direction.

  - o If I don't have a specific suggestion from the passenger I just start moving and watch the GPS application for the first navigation direction.

  - o Yes, sometimes after I start moving it will become obvious turning around would have made more sense, but I go easy on myself and sometimes will say: *"Looks like it makes more sense to turn around"* then I turn the car around.

  Sometimes situations like these are an opportunity for a shared laugh between you and a new passenger. I'll say something like: *"Oh I could have turned around, it would have been easier or faster."*

  - o Don't take yourself too seriously. Remember your primary goal – making money.

  - o After all, we're not talking about adding 5 minutes to the trip, just a few seconds.

- If a passenger suggests a different route, unless you are certain about the route and want to tell the passenger why... just take their suggestion without showing any sign of frustration. You will get paid for the trip without regard to the route.
  - o You may be surprised to hear many rideshare drivers take it very personally when a passenger suggests a different route and these drivers will react very negatively to navigation suggestions from passengers. I hear this said about other drivers all the time from my passengers. Again, over-asserting your ego is probably not going to serve you well as a rideshare driver.

  - o It makes no sense to me drivers would care. Why are these drivers taking directions so personally and/or why are they attempting to "train" a passenger they probably will never see again?

o Most importantly, at least from my way of thinking, why are these drivers setting up an uncomfortable situation with the passengers in their car?

Common sense is a very helpful tool for a rideshare driver, don't start a conversation you may not enjoy unless it is very important to you.

Reacting negatively to passenger navigation suggestions violates at least four of the suggestions in this book:

o Stay neutral, what happens is only "good" or "bad" because of your thinking;

o Don't agitate passengers and create an uncomfortable situation with the strangers in your car;

o It's not your job to train passengers to behave 'better' during their next rideshare trip, focus on what you want the current trip to be like;

o Most importantly stay focused on your primary goal, making money, everything else is secondary.

• **The next hot tip to "Drive like a pro from you first trip:" don't "run at the mouth" with every passenger.**

Some passengers want to have conversations. Some don't.

o Remember, you and your passengers are strangers and you know nothing about them; what mood they are in; what happened to them before they entered your car; etc.

The TNC's stories in your email inbox will often share examples about rideshare drivers telling funny stories or jokes or in some way going out of their way to entertain passengers; getting "Golden Fist bumps" at the end of every ride; etc.

Be yourself and make your own choices how you want to behave!

Doing anything else is going to eventually get "old" so be yourself from your very first trip.

- o In my personal life I don't initiate fist bumps with my friends, so I don't do them as a rideshare driver either.

- o In my twenties I was a waiter for over 7 years, it took 6 years of waiting tables full-time before I realized my job responsibilities did not include being the entertainer; people want you to bring them food and drinks efficiently. This is the restaurant customer's primary goal for their waitperson, being an entertainer will always be a secondary goal if it's even on the customer's list at all.

- o At the beginning of the trip you might want to say something about the weather (or similar generic comment) which communicates that you are open to conversation, then shut up unless the passenger keeps the conversation going.

- After two years as a rideshare driver I sometimes see the destination location and say: *"Oh we're going to Joe's Crab Shack on Sheridan!"*; a spontaneous comment because I've been to that drop-off location before.

  - o It occurred to me one day that I could use this kind of comment as a way to suggest that I was an experienced driver even when I was new to the gig.

  - o If something I've said proves to be wrong, for example at the beginning of the trip I've said: *"Oh, Joe's Crab Shack is next to that bridal shop."* Then when we get to the destination and Joe's is clearly not next to a bridal shop. I don't worry about it or say anything correcting my previous remarks... our experiences as human beings are primarily about perception not reality.

  - o My primary goal is making money with everything else secondary.

Don't try to create the "perfect" things to say at the start of every trip.

> Once when I was traveling as a passenger I asked the rideshare driver a question soon after entering the car and after answering my question he said: *"I didn't get a chance to deliver my spiel."*
>
> o   As a fellow rideshare driver I was of course interested what he said to every passenger so said: *"I'm sorry please do give me your spiel."*
>
> o   His prepared speech talked about requesting the car be warmer or cooler; the fact that he had bottled water and mints; if I had music requests please ask...
>
> o   Maybe because I spent so many years as a waiter who was required to deliver the same "pitch" with every customer I am unwilling to have a rideshare driver prepared speech.
>
> o   After a few dozen rides any kind of prepared speech is going to get old for you and I think prepared speeches tend to communicate you are new at rideshare driving... I suspect most seasoned drivers are not delivering a prepared speech at the beginning of ever passenger trip.

This is an appropriate time to point out you can try most anything, if you don't like it then stop, it's always up to you, your car, your day, your experience.

- **Don't try to be overly friendly, unfortunately appearing to be a little too enthusiastic about being essentially a taxi driver tends to identify that you are new to the job.** The restaurant Joe's Crab Shack expects waiters and waitresses to line up and dance, if this were not an expectation it's unlikely their waitstaff would go to these lengths to be entertaining. Rideshare driving is your gig, you make the calls, do what feels right to you.

- **Go easy on yourself.** Likely as not even though you feel "new" it does not show to your passengers because you learned how to "Drive like a pro from your first trip" by reading this book and taking some of the suggestions in this section.

Put your focus on the basic nature of the job... transporting passengers safely from Point A to Point B.

When I was a new driver I often noticed tension in my body for no particular reason, except that transporting strangers in my personal car is not a "normal" experience for me or any new rideshare driver.

- It took months of rideshare driving and hundreds (if not thousands) of trips before I felt completely comfortable transporting strangers in my car and even now a trip will sometimes feel "odd" even though often I can't define an exact reason why.

MUSIC

After spending months trying to play music I believed my passengers would enjoy, I decided to play music I know I will enjoy, and hopefully my passengers will enjoy too.

For example, I like Led Zeppelin, but I don't have any of their songs on the music playlists I use. Led Zeppelin's songs were never mainstream, you had to like that kind of music.

Once a passenger asked if I had any Led Zeppelin and I wished I had a hard rock playlist ready to go because I love most hard rock music from the 1970s.

People who, for example, listen only to rap or reggae music will be disappointed by the music in my car no matter what I am currently playing, and I am ok with that.

I play mainstream, popular music mostly from the 1980s & 1990s and I don't try to cater to everyone's individual music tastes, if for no other reason because I don't know what my passenger's musical preferences are and I'm not willing to ask because I'm not willing to have every kind of music available and distract myself from driving trying to queue up the "perfect" music.

Remember most of your passengers are taking rideshare transportation because the price seems right, in other words cheap. I'm not willing to work hard to deliver unnecessary "perks" for bargain shoppers, no offense intended, I am an avid bargain shopper I'm just being practical about how I want to spend my rideshare driving days.

Typically, I am not going to search for a song among the thousands of songs in my MP3 player or do anything that takes my eyes off the road and/or distracts me from doing "the job" which is always driving safely from Point A to Point B.

Rarely a passenger asks if I have a certain song or type of music, the rare request is not worth taking my eyes off the road and risking the safety of the trip. Maybe the passenger will only give me four stars because I didn't play DJ exactly to their tastes, oh well.

One of my playlists is rarely used but when I get a parent traveling with kids under 5 years old my kid's playlist tends to distract the young ones which I hope helps my fellow parents have a more enjoyable trip, and hopefully a relaxing moment with the kids entertained.

Sometimes I get tired of listening to the same songs over and over but usually if passengers are in my car I think of the music playing like music on an elevator, it's background music, who cares if it's the same song I heard an hour ago, this is my "job" I'm on the road to earn.

I don't use the same phone running the TNC applications to play music for a number of reasons, including not wanting a streaming music application potentially disrupting the TNC driver application behavior or interfering with the GPS application navigation. I like the spoken GPS navigation directions and if music were coming from the same device then: "Turn right on Main Street" will play over my music system speakers.

The TNCs offer passengers the option to control the music played during their trip by having an integration to Pandora or other online music applications.

I have never signed up for these music integrations, again most passengers are bargain shopping for the cheapest ride I don't see it as my job to go out of my way to cater to individual tastes, also I don't want a streaming music application interfering with the TNC driver applications, sometimes the TNC applications will freeze up, crash, and do "funny" things even without having unnecessary applications running at the same time.

The TNC driver applications don't need help being buggy, and if you have an issue and are contacting TNC support they may ask: "What other applications are you running on your phone?"

Tell support you're playing music and I'm betting the response you'll hear is: "*Don't do that.*"

Remember, most trips are less than 10 minutes long and as rideshare drivers we're not planning the perfect wedding reception, we are transporting passengers safely from Point A to Point B.

While allowing passengers the option to control the music might be a nice thing for the passengers, in my experience most passengers who want to control the music seem to want to play songs where, at least to me, have the primary goal of seeing if the songs will "get a rise" out of the rideshare driver.

You may think I'm kidding but almost every time I have let passenger's control the music in my car they play rap songs with misogynistic, violent, and sexual lyrics.

Thank you, not interested, and I'm not the entertainment I am your driver.

Also true: for a 5-minute trip where I make less than four dollars, passengers expecting to control the music played in the car are expecting too much. The TNCs may have fostered this kind of passenger expectation but I don't work for the TNCs, I am a private contractor with 100% discretion how I choose to safely transport passengers from Point A to Point B.

In my car I have the ability to let passengers connect their phones to my music system, commonly referred to as an "Aux Cord" connection.

If I pick up passengers on a long ride, perhaps to a concert venue (Red Rocks Amphitheater is one of the best concert venues in the world and on the western edge of Denver Metro area so typically a longer ride) I will often offer my Aux cable saying: *"Does anyone want to play D.J.?"*

I want passengers to have the best trip possible, within reason, and I say what's reasonable. I enjoy giving great customer service, it makes me feel good about me.

When passengers ask to plug into my Aux cable I will usually let them, why not, unless it is a really short ride then I politely say: "No" because what's the point?

I am not exaggerating at all when I say passengers seem to play songs with misogynistic, violent, controversial content, and/or sexual lyrics typically rap music and they want to play it loud. Again, thank you no, I'm not interested.

I am a musician and I enjoy almost all kinds of "quality" music from most music genres; but I'm not interested in being part of a passenger's entertainment if they think trying to annoy the rideshare driver is entertaining.

Solo passengers are less likely to want to control the music, after all what's the fun of hassling the rideshare driver if your friends aren't there to admire the results?

I have a high-quality sound system in my car, it can be turned up really loud with zero distortion.

Also true, loud music can be really distracting from paying attention to the road and safety is a basic "job" requirement.

If I'm playing my music and a passenger requests I "Crank up that song" I will typically show off my premium audio system, it rocks!

When I have loaned out my Aux cord connection to a passenger in the front seat, they will sometimes help themselves to the volume control and turn the music up loud.

If this happens I just turn it down without saying anything, I decide what's "reasonable" behavior in my car. When I've turned the music down no one has ever protested but if they did... I would likely say as little as possible and might even ignore protests.

My car, my rules, nothing to discuss.

CONCLUSION

I prefer short goodbyes so not going to attempt to tie the whole book together in a flowery conclusion.

If you choose to give rideshare driving a try send an email to wylee@RideshareBusinessGuide.com and I'll respond personally answering your questions and if you like provide information about our new driver mentor program.

If you are a new driver and sign up for Lyft or Uber using my New Driver Referral ID, I will provide 90 days free mentorship through live phone calls, emails, and text.

If you haven't read Driving for Uber and Lyft - How Much Can Drivers Earn? yet, I think you will find this companion book well worth the investment of your time and money.

Be sure to check out the website www.RideshareBusinessGuide.com and get meaningful responses to the latest rideshare driving news stories.

So again, thank you for reading *How to Be a Lyft and Uber Driver – The Unofficial Driver's Manual*, I believe you now know more than most drivers with over 2,500 lifetime trips and will benefit with higher average rideshare driving income and I sincerely hope greater peace of mind.

For now, here's wishing you safe travels on your journeys and it is my greatest hope you value your life and live it well.

~Wylee, a.k.a. "YMAN" or just "Y."

Made in the USA
Coppell, TX
22 April 2023

15942296R00111